W9-CSG-053

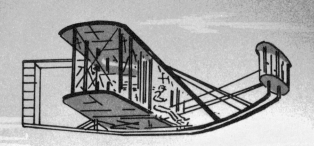

All About
Famous Inventors and Their Inventions

More than fifty of the greatest inventions of all time are described in this book, from the wheel and the jib sail to submarines and frozen foods.

Fletcher Pratt tells of ingenious men and women, their ideas, and their remarkable achievements.

Mr. Pratt, who died in 1956, was the author of more than forty books.

All About Famous Inventors and Their Inventions

allabout
books

By Fletcher Pratt

Illustrated by Rus Anderson

RANDOM HOUSE
NEW YORK

COPYRIGHT 1955 BY FLETCHER PRATT

All rights reserved under International and Pan-American Copyright Conventions. Published in New York by Random House, Inc., and simultaneously in Toronto, Canada, by Random House of Canada, Limited.

LIBRARY OF CONGRESS CATALOG CARD NUMBER: 54-7008

MANUFACTURED IN THE UNITED STATES OF AMERICA

5   1064

CONTENTS

INTRODUCTION

Human beings have always searched for ways to make their lives more pleasant. From the very beginning, men have tried to find easier and quicker ways to do their work. As a result, man no longer lives in caves, but in comfortable homes. He now travels in airplanes and trains, instead of on foot.

This kind of progress has been made possible by inventions. The first man who sharpened a piece of flint and then attached it to a stick had a better weapon than the stick alone. Simple as this weapon was, it was a true invention. Some time later, other men discovered that a boat could be pushed through the water more rapidly when a carefully shaped paddle was used instead of a plain board. That, too, was an invention.

Inventions are important to each of us, for we use hundreds of them every day. In fact, they are considered so valuable that all governments give inventors a document called a patent. To obtain this, the inventor must first prove that he has really found something new. After he receives the patent he will be the only person allowed to manufacture his invention for a number of years. If it is a good one, its inventor will earn a great deal of money because he will be its only producer.

Most of the inventions described in this book are fairly modern, but this does not mean that earlier peoples were not successful inventors. However, their inventions were few in number because they lacked proper tools and scientific knowledge.

One of the very earliest and most important inventions was the wheel, which made it easy to carry heavy loads over rough ground. None of our modern machines could have been invented if the wheel had not been devised first. Because the American Indians never succeeded in inventing the wheel, their civilization never progressed very far. The natives of Australia failed to invent either the wheel or the bow, and they were held back still more.

One of the main reasons why the ancient Egyptians became civilized so long ago was that some clever man among them invented the water-wheel. This was a kind of pump for carrying the waters of the Nile into the fields. Another ancient Egyptian invented a boat that would easily transport heavy loads up and down the river.

Although we do not usually think of the Greeks, the

Romans, or the Chinese as great inventors, they thought out many familiar and useful devices. The Greeks invented the arch, which enables us to build bridges across streams and to erect large buildings with open spaces. The Romans invented concrete, with which we can make stone in any size and shape we need. They also invented safety pins and pipes that heated houses in much the same way as our radiators do. The Chinese invented rockets and the compass.

Then came the long period known as the "Dark Ages," when scarcely anything at all was invented. This book begins with the end of the Dark Ages and brings the story of inventions down to the present. But the story is not finished. Probably at this very minute some man or woman is working on an invention that will be as important as anything that has ever been devised.

All About
Famous Inventors and Their Inventions

1

Explosives, Printing, and the Telescope

Men who lived during the Dark Ages knew a much different and simpler world than the one we know today. The changes that have taken place were largely the results of three inventions. Without these discoveries we should not be able to build tall buildings. We would not know how to fire a gun. There would be no way of getting enough fuel to keep our houses warm. We would have no means of learning how to cure many diseases. Also, books would be so expensive that very few people would ever read. We could never be certain what the moon and stars are really like.

The three inventions that made it possible for us to accomplish so much were these: explosives, printing, and the telescope.

The first explosive was gunpowder, but who its inventor was we do not know. At the time of its invention—the Middle Ages—people were fond of mixing things together to see what would happen. What was more natural than that some curious individual should mix three common substances: saltpeter, sulphur and charcoal! Saltpeter can be found under

Roger Bacon experimented with gunpowder

any manure pile and was always easy to get. So was sulphur, which is found wherever there are volcanoes. And of course charcoal was found in every household.

The first man who told us about the experiment was Roger Bacon, an English friar who was curious about everything in nature. In 1242 he wrote a book in which he said he had combined saltpeter, sulphur and charcoal and then applied fire to it. The result was a flash and a sound a little like thunder. We would call it an explosion.

Although it would seem from this that Friar Bacon had discovered gunpowder, he does not usually get the credit

4

for being its inventor. For that matter, he does not deserve it. Many people who invented or discovered things for which they could think of no practical use wrote about their discoveries and then forgot about them. So it was with Roger Bacon. He was interested in seeing his mixture explode, but he never tried to put the explosion to work.

The man who thought of using the gunpowder seems to have been another friar named Berthold Schwartz. He lived at Freiburg in Germany, a hundred years after Roger Bacon's time. Schwartz had the idea of putting some of this mixture into an iron tube which was closed at one end except for a tiny hole through which a flame could be applied to the powder. He then put a stone ball on top of the mixture. When the powder was lit it exploded, and out shot the stone ball! Berthold Schwartz had invented guns.

This was an important invention. Before people had guns, the victory in a battle usually went to the side that had the greatest number of men. One reason for the fall of the Roman Empire was that there were not enough Romans to keep back the wild tribesmen from the North. But after Friar Bacon and Friar Schwartz had done their work, it became possible for a small number of men who were armed with guns to keep back a large number of fighters who were armed only with spears or swords. The United States could never have been settled if the settlers had had no guns with which to keep off the Indians.

The invention of gunpowder was also important in another way. Before it was discovered, a rich baron in his suit of armor could beat down any number of people who could not afford such a coating. He could even sit comfortably in his stone castle, knowing that nobody could get at him. After the gun was invented, neither the armor nor the castle was a protection to him. The two friars had made it possible for people to live peaceably without worrying lest everything they owned be carried away by a robber baron.

This was not all that the invention of gunpowder did. Before it was discovered, men had to use chisels or picks or other hand tools to get rocks out of the earth. Digging up stones required such an immense amount of work that only churches or government buildings or the homes of the rich could be constructed of stone. But when rocks could be blown apart by explosives, it became possible for almost anyone to have a stone house.

Today nearly everything that comes from under the ground reaches us with the help of explosives. Coal, iron, aluminum, and all other metals must be blown loose from the rocks in which they lie hidden. They would be very expensive and very scarce if it were not for the work of Friar Bacon and Friar Schwartz.

But the explosives that do so much work for us today are a long way from gunpowder. Another step forward was made 500 years after Berthold Schwartz lighted gunpowder in an iron tube and 600 years after Roger Bacon made his flash and thunder-like sound. This advance took place when an Italian named Ascanio Sobrero tried the old game of putting things together to see what would happen. He combined two substances called nitric acid and glycerine, and got a pale liquid which was named nitroglycerine. The new

6

substance proved to be very explosive, going off with several times the force of gunpowder.

Sobrero, like Roger Bacon, was a man who enjoyed experiments for their own sake and was not much interested in what use was made of them. Later, his nitroglycerine was tried by other people who found that it made a fine explosion. They also discovered that it was very dangerous to handle and often exploded when its container was jarred. When it was used for blasting rocks another disadvantage became apparent. Nitroglycerine, being a liquid, was apt to run away into cracks in the rocks before a fuse could be attached to light it.

In the nineteenth century, a Swedish chemist named Alfred Nobel began to look for some way of putting nitroglycerine to work. He believed that it would be safer and easier to handle if he could mix it with a dry substance that would take up the liquid.

Alfred Nobel tried all sorts of things. He mixed jelly with the nitroglycerine and this did fairly well, but it did not burn well. He tried wood shavings and charcoal, but they were not of much help in making nitroglycerine safer to handle. The wood shavings caused the trouble this time, because sometimes nitroglycerine will go off by itself if it is touching anything that is grown out of the ground.

Then, as often happens, the solution popped up unexpectedly. Cans of nitroglycerine came to Nobel packed in a very light substance called *kieselguhr*, which is very common in Sweden and Northern Germany. It is made of the remains of the shells of tiny sea animals of thousands of years ago. In 1876 Alfred Nobel tried using some of this packing material to take up the nitroglycerine.

This proved the right thing at last. *Kieselguhr* took up a lot of nitroglycerine, and when it was wet with the explosive it could be pressed together into sticks. These were easy and safe to carry. When one of the sticks was placed in a hole bored in a rock it would blow the rock apart. Alfred Nobel named his invention dynamite. It was the first of what are called the "high explosives." Today there are many others and they have many uses, but they all go back to Alfred Nobel's dynamite. It would be hard to build most of our dams or tunnels without the high explosives. They are also used in mining.

Alfred Nobel lived a happy life and became very rich as the result of his invention. After his death his money was used to give yearly prizes for the best work in chemistry, medicine, physics, literature, and the promotion of peace. Nobel prizes are being awarded to this very day.

Johannes Gutenberg, a German printer, was not so successful in achieving recognition for his invention of a new method of printing. Early in the fifteenth century he worked in the mint of the city of Mainz in Germany, cutting the dies from which coins were stamped. He never seems to have had much money, and was always borrowing, usually for some scheme to get rich quickly. About 1430 he left Mainz for Strasbourg to go into business as a polisher of stones. When this project did not succeed, Johannes Gutenberg began looking around for something else.

Sometime around 1448 he was back in Mainz working on a new idea. He had thought of a way to print books. In those days most books produced in Europe were written out by hand. This made them very expensive. Some books were printed from wooden blocks on which had been carved the pictures and letters that would be stamped on the various pages. The Chinese had printed by this process for centuries. But it was a long slow method, for every letter had to be carved on each block by hand.

Now in his business as a jeweler, Gutenberg frequently carved initials into stones. These were used as seals to stamp initials in the soft wax that had been dropped on a document. Sometimes ink would be rubbed on a seal. Then the initials could be stamped onto paper.

It occurred to Gutenberg that if he had a large number of separate carved letters, they could be moved around and made up into words and sentences and pages. He realized that it would take a very long time to carve from metal all the letters he would need, so at first he carved his letters from wood. By pressing the wooden letters into sand and then pouring liquid metal into the spaces that had been made in the sand, he was able to make as many molded letters as he wanted.

These separate letters could be moved to make any combination of words. Then they could be moved again to make new words in another printing job. Gutenberg is generally regarded as the first printer in Europe to use movable type.

The first metal he used was brass. After the letters were

cast, they had to be polished and finished by hand. Unfortunately, they were not very even. Still worse, when Gutenberg inked them and printed with them, he had to use so much pressure that the soft brass was banged out of shape. Although his idea had worked and he was printing from movable type, he could print only a few copies with one set of letters.

Next he tried hammering the letters into lead instead of into sand. He then used the lead as a mold for casting the type to be used in printing. This was a good method, because the letters cast in the lead mold did not need so much polishing as those cast in sand. But still the type was so soft that it got battered in the press, and Gutenberg had to spend more time making type than in printing.

He tried different mixtures of tin and lead in his types and meanwhile printed a few things. Then, as usual, he ran out of money. This was about 1450, but the inventor was not long in finding a rich banker named Johann Fust who agreed to pay Gutenberg enough to live on for several years. About this time he printed his first book. It was in Latin and told how to make speeches. There were twenty-eight pages, each of which was printed separately, so the buyers had to bind them together for themselves.

Gutenberg was so pleased with his success that he immediately went to work printing a Bible. This was a bold thing to do, for the Bible is a very large book. Furthermore, Gutenberg had not worked out all the details of making and using his movable type.

Then, five years after the first loan from Fust, the banker began to ask for his money—but there wasn't any.

In the fifteenth century Gutenberg printed his first book

How could anyone make money on printing books when so few people knew how to read? So Fust sued Gutenberg and the inventor had to turn over his type, his press, his tools, and his paper. Fust gave them to another die-cutter named Peter Schöpffer, who made great improvements in the method of casting type. Many people consider him quite as important as Gutenberg.

In 1465 Gutenberg was given a post at the court of the Archbishop of Mainz, with a new suit of clothes every year. His duties do not seem to have included any printing, and not long afterward he died. Nobody thought of him as a great inventor at the time. In fact, so little interest was shown in him that we do not know what he looked like or whether he was married. Still, it is hard to see how the modern world could be what it is without the work of Johannes Gutenberg.

Like many inventions, the telescope was one in which several people had a hand, but it is to an Italian named Galileo Galilei that most of the credit belongs.

Galileo was born in Pisa, the son of a father who was clever at both mathematics and music, but who was always poor because he could never make any money at either pursuit. As a result, the older Galilei, deciding that his son should not enter such poorly paying businesses, sent him to the University of Pisa to learn to be a doctor.

While still a student Galileo Galilei made the first of his great discoveries—that no matter whether a pendulum swings a long distance or a short distance, each swing takes the same

Galileo dropped two objects from the Leaning Tower of Pisa

length of time. This did not immediately lead to any invention, but it showed that Galileo had a good mind. A little later he happened into a classroom where a lecture on geometry was being given. This excited him so much that he insisted on being allowed to study mathematics. In three years he had advanced so far that he was giving lectures himself.

At that time scientists believed that if a heavy object and a light object were dropped from a height at the same time, the heavy one would reach the ground first. Galileo proved by mathematics that this belief must be wrong. Then he climbed to the top of the famous Leaning Tower of Pisa and dropped from it two objects of different weights. They both struck the ground at the same time!

Galileo also demonstrated that other mathematical theories were wrong. When he laughed at the men who believed in them, he made many enemies. On one occasion he said that a machine being built to dredge the harbor of Leghorn would not work. It failed just as he had foretold, but his warning made him very unpopular. Things became so unpleasant that he left Pisa and went to Padua.

In Padua, which at that time belonged to the Republic of Venice, there was a famous University at which Galileo began to give lectures on mathematics. He was already famous and people came to listen to him in such great numbers that the University had to build a special hall holding two thousand persons. While he was at Padua Galileo invented the first thermometer and an instrument that is still used in making geometrical drawings.

His most famous invention began in 1609, when he heard from a traveler that a Belgian named Hans Lippershey had invented a glass that would make distant objects look as though they were near by. The traveler said Lippershey had done this by combining a convex lens with a concave one— that is, both lenses had one flat side and one curved side. But the convex lens curved out on one side and the concave lens curved *in*.

When Galileo heard of this idea, he spent an entire night thinking about the mathematical principles of Lippershey's telescope. The next morning he started to build one by placing two lenses at the ends of a lead tube. The very first one he built was much better than Lippershey's, even though Galileo had never seen that one.

At once he began to improve his first model and to sell telescopes. Eventually he made hundreds of them with his own hands and sent them all over Europe. The Republic of Venice was so delighted with his discovery that it raised his salary to three times the amount that any other professor had ever received.

It is not only because Galileo was a good mathematician and mechanic that he is considered one of the greatest scientists of history. It is also because of the use he made of his telescope. In those days nearly everybody believed that the earth was the center of the universe, and that the sun, planets and stars revolved around it. The Milky Way was considered to be simply a band of light in the heavens, and the moon was thought to be flat.

When Galileo looked through his telescope he saw that none of these beliefs was true. He observed that the moon had mountains, that the sun was spinning on its axis, and that the planet Jupiter had moons like the one that moves around the earth. He saw that the Milky Way was made up of separate stars.

Galileo wrote a book in which he told about his observations. They proved, he said, that the earth was really a small planet that moved around the sun with the other planets. Some of his enemies complained to the authorities of the Catholic Church that Galileo's statements contradicted the Bible. Galileo had to go to Rome and defend himself. He did this so well that he was held blameless, but he was told

Galileo and his telescope

not to write in such a way again.

Galileo went back to his lectures and his telescopes but he could not stop thinking that the earth really did move around the sun. In another book which he wrote sixteen years later he proved this fact, but added that it did not contradict anything in the Bible. In the same book he was even more sarcastic about his enemies than he had been when he was younger. This time they could prove he had written in a way he had been told not to. He was forced to say publicly that the earth did not move after all.

Probably he did not care very much. His new telescopes were everywhere now and anyone who cared to use one of them could see for himself that everything Galileo had said was perfectly true. He lived to be a very old man and went blind. But he never stopped thinking about mathematics and new inventions, and went on dictating his ideas to his pupils. The most famous men in the world came to see and honor him.

2

From the Jib Sail to the Airplane

We know that the man who made the first great invention in transportation was Dutch—and that is all we do know about him. There is reason to believe that he lived at about the time America was being discovered. This is fortunate, for if it were not for this nameless Dutchman, Columbus' discovery would never have done anyone much good.

Before that time, most ships had only square sails. This meant that although they could sail very well when the wind came from behind them and pushed them along, there was no possible way of sailing against the wind. Also, when the wind came from the side of a ship—abeam, as it is called—a lot of its force was spent in pushing the ship sidewise instead of straight ahead.

On the ocean this was a serious matter. Because the earth spins on its axis, and because there are no mountains at sea to change the direction of the winds, they blow steadily from one direction for many days at a time. In the part of the Atlantic crossed by Columbus these steady winds are from the northeast. They easily carried him to the New World, but the trip back took him nearly twice as long and he had to go far out of his way.

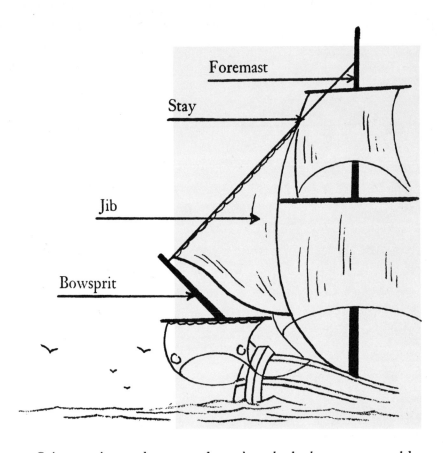

Foremast

Stay

Jib

Bowsprit

Other early explorers and settlers had the same trouble. Ships were continuously landing in the wrong places because they had to move in the direction in which the wind blew. It was quite clear that unless some way of solving this difficulty were found, there could be no real settlement of the New World nor any real trade between the New World and the Old.

The Dutchman who solved the problem was probably not thinking of crossing the Atlantic at all. He was interested

20

in making his ship behave better in the waters around the coast of his own country, where the winds are very uncertain.

To understand his invention you must know that at the forward end of sailing ships there is a spar called the bowsprit. Its principal use at that time was to furnish a place to attach the strong rope from the top of the foremast. This rope, which is called the stay, holds the foremast in place. On the bowsprit there was usually hung a little square sail which was not of much use. The unknown Dutchman thought of hanging a very much bigger triangular sail from the stay.

When he did this, he had invented the jib. People probably laughed at him because most sailors don't like to see things change, but it was not long before they began to realize how very important this change was. They found that the jib, far out over the end of the ship, gave a very strong pull. If it were properly set it would keep the ship from drifting sidewise when the wind was abeam.

A ship that carried a jib could even be sailed in a direction fairly close to the one from which the wind was coming. Also, with the help of the rudder—a piece of wood by which the vessel was steered—this new jib allowed a ship to change her direction very rapidly. That is, her captain could sail in a direction a little to the right of the direction of the wind, then change over and sail a little to the left. This is called "tacking" and it makes it possible to sail against the wind.

After jibs were invented, it became possible for sailing

After jibs were invented, ships could sail against the wind

ships to go wherever they pleased, and so regular colonies could be set up in America. We know jibs were invented around 1527 and in Holland, because a picture of that date shows a Dutch ship with the new sails. It is the first picture that shows them. But we do not know who owned the ship.

The next great inventor was not aware that his new discovery would eventually be used in transportation. He was James Watt, a young Scot who learned to make different kinds of instruments by working at night while he was earning his living. When he was just twenty-one the College of Glasgow employed him to repair its telescopes and other instruments. A few years later, in 1764, someone gave him a model of a steam engine to repair.

It was the only kind of steam engine known in those days, and it had no other use but to pump water out of mines. Even for this it was not particularly good, because it worked slowly and burned so much fuel that it was expensive to run. In fact, it was a good deal like Roger Bacon's gunpowder— an interesting discovery, but not very practical.

Before this time, James Watt had been talking with the college professors about how steam might be used. He had even tried one or two experiments, but without much success. But the moment he looked at the model of a pumping engine he knew why it worked so badly.

You probably know the principle of steam engines. It is this: when water is boiled and changes into steam, the steam needs much more space than the water requires. Steam is powerful, too. It can push with great force.

In the engine that Watt examined, steam was let into a cylinder, where it pushed a piston to the end of the cylinder. Then cold water was sprayed into the cylinder. This cooled the steam to water, and as it no longer took up so much room, the pressure of the air on the other end of the piston was enough to drive it back up, ready for the next dose of steam.

The trouble was that at each stroke of the piston, the water cooled off the cylinder and it took a lot of steam and time to heat it up again. James Watt saw that if he could find a way of keeping the cylinder hot all the time, the engine would work much faster and not use up so much steam. He began studying everything there was to know about steam.

James Watt developed a condenser for the steam engine

From the Jib Sail to the Airplane

One day, while Watt was walking through a park on a Sunday afternoon, the right idea suddenly came to him. If a space connected with the cylinder could be emptied of air, the steam would flow into it and could be cooled there, away from the cylinder. The thing to do then was to make a separate chamber in which the steam would be cooled and condensed. This would also help draw the piston down the cylinder while steam was coming in.

Of course, there had to be a valve that would open when it was time for the steam to be drawn out of the cylinder and a pump to empty the condenser, but these were not hard to build. James Watt added a jacket filled with steam around his cylinder to keep it still hotter, and then built a model of his engine. It worked just as he expected. Although there were several of the old pumping engines using steam before James Watt, this one has always been thought of as the real beginning of the steam engine.

Excellent as Watt's engine was, it still needed improvements. But its inventor was not very strong, and for this reason he could not give as much time as he wished to his wonderful new engine. He even went into debt buying parts, and the businessman he took in as a partner lost all his money before Watt's engine could be made to work properly. Watt then found a new partner named Boulton and kept on working. In 1775, ten years from the time when the idea first came to him in the park, the firm of Boulton and Watt really began building steam engines.

For many years they were used only to pump out mines. This was an important work, for many of the mines in western England were filling up with water so rapidly that the old pumping engines could not clear them. Furthermore, the old engines used so much fuel that it often did not pay to use them. James Watt's engines used much less fuel and were so much better and faster that soon all the mine owners in England and other countries were buying them.

Still, James Watt was not satisfied. He kept inventing new parts to make his engines better. Five years after producing the first successful pumping engine he found a way to make the up-and-down motion of the piston rod turn a wheel. Soon after that Watt began putting all the working parts of the engine in a jacket so that steam would come in on both sides of the piston, first on one side and then on the other side.

One by one he invented nearly all the parts that go into a modern steam engine. He lived a very long time, long enough to see his engines being used not only for pumping but also for driving machines in many kinds of factories. Bit by bit, these machines took over the work that used to be done by hand.

Meanwhile, Watt had become famous. He had friends all over the world to whom he wrote many letters and from whom he got numbers of new ideas. He studied medicine, architecture, music, and law, and wrote letters to people about all these things. When he was over seventy he learned a number of languages.

One day in Watt's old age there came to call on him a young American artist named Robert Fulton. The son of poor parents, Fulton had been unable to go to school, but he went to work for a jeweler from whom he learned a great deal about machines. As a boy Fulton was known as "Quicksilver Bob" because he used all his money to buy quicksilver for his experiments.

To such an interested young man, James Watt was glad to show his engines and the models for new ones. Probably the young artist told the old inventor that he had very little money, for not long afterwards Robert Fulton was doing surveying and engineering for some people Watt knew. Fulton found this work so pleasant that he gave up painting to spend all his time working with machines.

Now that people had Watt's engine to furnish power, a great many things began to be done by machines. Robert Fulton was one of the people who invented new ones. He invented a machine for sawing marble and one for making ropes. Neither of these was very important, but then he became interested in the idea of a submarine.

Fulton heard that the French government was interested in this idea too, so he went to Paris. In France he built his submarine, and dived with it to a depth of 25 feet, where he stayed for an hour. Although this was the first submarine that worked, Fulton is not really the inventor of the submarine, because his boat had to be moved by a man turning a crank.

The really important point about Fulton's visit to France was that he met the American ambassador, Robert Livingston. Fulton explained to Livingston what he had learned from James Watt about steam engines. Then he told Liv-

In 1807 Fulton's Clermont, *the first practical steamship,*

ingston about his belief that such an engine could be used to move a ship.

The idea of using a steam engine in a ship had been tried on a canal in Scotland, but it had not been successful. Fulton thought he knew what was wrong—the ship had been pushed by one paddle-wheel at the stern. This had interfered with the steering, and much of the engine's power had been lost in getting it to the wheel. Fulton suggested that two paddle-wheels be used, one on each side of the ship. Such a vessel would be especially useful on rivers, where it was hard for sailing ships to do well.

Livingston encouraged Fulton, who built a small steamship according to his own ideas. He had to invent almost

28

made her maiden voyage on the Hudson River

as many parts for it as James Watt had invented for his engine. After all, Fulton's engine would have to be different from the engines that were used on land, where there was plenty of room for everything. On land, too, there were no worries about keeping the fires under the boilers away from the sides of a wooden ship.

At last Fulton's boat was built and it steamed up and down the river Seine. Although it was only a model like Watt's first steam engine, Livingston and Fulton were pleased. As soon as they got back to America they started work on a much bigger ship.

This new vessel was called the *Clermont,* after Livingston's home. She started up the Hudson in 1807 and kept right

on going, to the surprise of the large crowd that had expected to see her carried away by the current. This was
the first practical steamship, and Fulton deserves all the credit
for it. Seven years later he built the first steam warship, but
she never got a chance to prove how good she was.

The success of the *Clermont* and other steamships set
people wondering whether steam engines might not be used
to move vehicles on land as well as on water. One of these
people was a young Englishman named George Stephenson,
whose job it was to take care of a pumping engine at the
Tillingworth coal mine. He had less education than Robert
Fulton and did not even know how to read. But he was so
anxious to learn about engines that at the age of eighteen he
started going to night school, learning reading, arithmetic,
and studying engines all at once. Four years later he had
gone ahead so fast that he was placed in charge of all the
engines at the Tillingworth Mine.

While there, he heard of some experiments being carried
out with "steam carriages"—engines intended to move about
the streets with passengers. They worked fairly well, but the
idea did not seem a good one to Stephenson. The steam carriages did not behave well on the rutted dirt roads of those
days, and the engine could carry very few passengers.

Now at the Tillingworth Mine the coal had to be carried
to a point about eight miles away to be shipped by water.
This was done by means of what was called a tramway—a
set of wooden rails with iron on top, on which ran cars
pulled by horses.

From the Jib Sail to the Airplane

George Stephenson persuaded the owners of the mine to let him build what he called a "traveling engine" to do the work of the horses. Building it was quite as much of a task as Fulton's steamboat had been. Nearly everything had to be made narrower than in a pumping engine, and all the parts had to be arranged differently. But George Stephenson worked it out, and on July 25, 1814, the first successful railroad engine began hauling cars of coal.

At this time a number of people began to think that passengers might be carried on tramways instead of in the stagecoaches that were then in use. How much better that would be than bumping along the rutty roads!

One such group set up a short tramway line between the towns of Stockton and Darlington. They intended to use horses to pull the coaches, but Stephenson heard of it and persuaded them to let him try his traveling engine. He had to take charge of laying the tracks so there would not be too many steep slopes, for the engine was not very strong. In 1825 the line was opened, with Stephenson himself driving the first train. Ahead of it galloped a man on horseback, waving a red flag to warn people the train was coming.

George Stephenson was so successful that when another group of men decided to build a tramway between the cities of Liverpool and Manchester, they hired Stephenson to put down the tracks. Not only was this a much longer line, but there were so many marshes and hills in the way that many of the best engineers said the line could not be laid at all. Nevertheless Stephenson succeeded in doing it.

The men who owned this tramway had intended to pull

Stephenson himself drove the first train.

the cars along it by means of fixed engines at various places hauling on cables. When George Stephenson did well at laying the track they changed their minds and agreed to hold a contest for the best locomotive engine.

Stephenson entered the contest with his engine, called the "Rocket." It was quite different from any engine ever built before, with a long boiler running along its side. Because the "Rocket" was much the best of the engines offered in the contest, the company ordered eight for its line. This was the first real railroad engine. Others that had been built up to that time were not much faster than a horse and had to

Ahead of it galloped a man on horseback.

stop every few miles for fuel and water, but the "Rocket" could make long trips and pull heavy loads.

The Liverpool and Manchester line was opened on September 15, 1830, and was such a success that people all over the world began to build railroads. Many of these were constructed by George Stephenson, who also built their engines.

One of the locomotives that Stephenson's "Rocket" beat in the contest was designed by John Ericsson, who invented so many things that his name will come up several times in this book. Ericsson was from Sweden, where he had worked at drawing maps for the army. For this he was paid double because he did twice as much work as anyone else. Ericsson had so many ideas for new pieces of machinery that in 1826 he went to England, where everybody was building new machines. Going into business as an engineer and inventor, he had no trouble in finding work, both at designing machines and their parts and at repairing machines that had broken down. He was especially good at making fine drawings, so that machines built from his designs worked out exactly right.

Among his many interests were ships and their engines. He thought that Robert Fulton's system of driving ships by paddle-wheels was very poor. The wheels were often damaged by objects floating in the water, and the large wheels were very hard to turn. Ericsson's idea was to place a large screw right under the stern of a ship. In a warship this would be especially useful because the engines could be placed below the water line. At that time they were still being carried on deck between the wheels, where a single shot would disable them.

People had had this idea before, but it never worked well. John Ericsson decided that this was because they had not studied the problems of how large the screw should be, what shape its blades should have, and how it should be connected to the engine. While working on other things he made the most careful calculations, and one day showed them to the American consul at Liverpool, a rich man named Francis Ogden.

Ogden agreed to help Ericsson build a small steamboat with one of his new propellers. It worked so well that Ogden

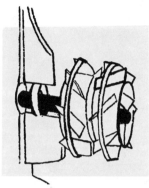

Ericsson's screw propeller

introduced Ericsson to Captain Robert Stockton of the U. S. Navy. Together, the three men built another screw propeller ship in 1839. It was such a success that Captain Stockton persuaded Ericsson to come to America and help design a new warship to be called the *Princeton*.

She was the first large ship to be driven by a screw. It succeeded because of John Ericsson's excellent drawings and his skill at engineering. After the *Princeton* was built she had an accident. For this Captain Stockton unjustly blamed John Ericsson, and saw to it that he was never paid for his services. Ericsson gave up working for the Navy. He turned his talents to inventing fire engines, and soon set up a business in New York.

As we have seen, the idea of using engines to carry people was thought of by several persons even before the invention of railroads. But several things got in the way of using engines on roads. It was not only that they were smoky and dirty. They frightened horses, and this was bad at a time when most people traveled on horseback or in coaches pulled by horses.

There was also trouble with the stagecoach owners, who realized that the use of engines on the highways would mean the end of their business. Eventually, in one country after another, these men managed to get laws passed forbidding the use of steam engines on roads. So the invention of the automobile had to wait for something else. One of the things it had to wait for was an Austrian railroad engineer named Julius Hock.

In the 1860s, when Julius Hock was working on engines, people were just beginning to use kerosene, a liquid made from the petroleum that comes from the ground. When kerosene is made, one of its by-products is the light oil we now call gasoline. Gasoline burns altogether too fast to be used for lighting, as was kerosene. In fact when gasoline is mixed with air it explodes.

The thought occurred to Julius Hock that although a big explosion causes much trouble, a very small one can be made to do useful work. If the explosion took place inside the cylinder of an engine, it would drive the piston. So in 1870 he built an engine in which air and a little light oil were sprayed into the cylinder of an engine. There a jet of flame set the mixture afire and produced a small explosion which drove the piston down. An arm attached to the piston pushed it up again, where it was ready for the next explosion.

Julius Hock never thought of using his engine to drive a vehicle. He was merely trying to make an engine that would stand in one place and furnish power for machines while

36

using the light oil that no one else wanted. His engine did this, but no one paid much attention to it, for there were several other kinds of engines that would do almost the same thing.

Then, about ten years later, a German engineer named Gottlieb Daimler began to wonder about using engines to drive vehicles on roads. His family had wanted him to be a town clerk, but while he was still in school he showed much more interest in machines than in books. At last his family agreed to apprentice him to a gun-maker. After that, Daimler worked hard all day and studied at night. When he became an engineer he did not take a day off for ten years on end. Sometimes he would get up in the night to work on designs. Then he would stay up till morning to see the sun rise and to hear the birds, of whom he was very fond.

As in the case of many great inventors, he solved his problems by thinking in ways that had not occurred to other men. He believed that nobody had been able to build a successful road vehicle moved by an engine because all the engines had been too large and heavy. None of the engines then in use would turn around more than 250 times, or revolutions, a minute. This was not fast enough to drive a vehicle unless both engine and vehicle were quite large.

Daimler thought if he could devise an engine that would turn a thousand revolutions a minute it could be made quite small and still drive some kind of vehicle. Other engineers told him he was wrong. They made calculations to show that if a steam engine were driven that fast it would blow up. This is because the pressure of steam does not change and if the engine parts were made thin and light they could not keep the steam from bursting the engine apart.

So Gottlieb Daimler began hunting for a kind of engine that could be made small and light and still turn very fast. In the course of this hunt he came on the patents of Julius Hock's engine. It seemed to him this would be just the thing, because the smaller the engine was made, the smaller the explosion in the cylinder would be.

There was just one difficulty. The jet of flame in the wall of Hock's cylinder often set off the explosion before it was really time. Gottlieb Daimler puzzled over this for a long time before he thought of running an electric current into the cylinder and making the electricity jump a gap where it gave off a spark to produce the explosion.

He was given a patent on his new engine in 1883. Two years later he mounted one on a bicycle and began to ride his gasoline-driven bike around the roads of Germany. Later still he founded a company which produced his new engine and became very prosperous. But though he invented the engine that made both the automobile and the airplane possible, he did not invent either one.

The trouble was that although Daimler got along well with his motorbicycle, he could not think of a way to get the power from the engine to the wheels of a four-wheel vehicle. He placed his engine between two rear wheels, but they got out of step with each other and he could not steer his car.

Then in 1887 there was an Exposition in Paris. A Frenchman whose name does not matter had seen one of Daimler's engines in a boat. The Frenchman wanted to show one like

One of the first automobiles made by Levassor

it at the Exposition, but he found that according to the rules it would have to be made in France. So he went to a firm that made machinery and sent Emil Levassor, a member of the firm, to get the engine design from Daimler.

The moment Levassor saw the boat he realized that Daimler had solved the problem of building an automobile, or "horseless carriage," as it was called then. He had placed his engine in the middle of the boat to make it balance, and carried the power back to the propeller through a spinning shaft. If the engine were placed at the front of the horseless carriage, the power could be carried back through a shaft in the same way. It would then be easy to make a gear that would turn both wheels equally and the steering could be done with the front wheels.

Levassor bought the French rights to Daimler's patents and built the vehicle he had planned. This was the first automobile. In looks, it was quite different from a modern automobile because it was built like a carriage with high wheels and iron tires. The steering was done with a rod that moved back and forth. Stranger still, it made a terrible noise as it bumped along, for the streets of Paris, where Levassor tried out his horseless carriage, were paved with cobblestones. But strange as it was, it had started a new page in the history of transportation. Credit for its invention must go to three men: Hock, Daimler, and Levassor.

While Levassor was making the first automobile, two young men in Dayton, Ohio, were busy making all sorts of things in whatever time they could spare from the bicycle shop they ran together. Although Wilbur and Orville Wright had been good students, their father, Bishop Wright, was unable to send them to college. So the two young men, who had always been interested in machines and machinery, decided to set up the bicycle shop together.

Orville Wright was the younger brother. When he was only seven years old someone gave him a toy helicopter that flew several feet in the air whenever it was wound up. This interested him so much that he tried to build bigger helicopters. Orville thought that if he made one big enough it would carry him into the air, but he found that the larger he made his helicopters, the worse they flew.

The boy did not understand why this was so, but his experiments with the helicopters increased his interest in flying. Because the only thing that came near to flying high was a kite, he began building and repairing kites, especially the big box kites which flew the best. His brother Wilbur did not take much interest in this activity, but whenever Orville needed help in working out some detail, he could get the help from his brother.

Not long after they opened their bicycle shop, the two brothers read about a German named Otto Lilienthal, who was making leaf-shaped gliders. Using these to launch himself off hilltops into the wind, he actually flew, sometimes for distances of several hundred feet. This news excited the Wright brothers. They read everything they could find about Lilienthal's experiments and built models of his gliders to be flown at the end of kite strings.

During these experiments, they found out several things. One was that a glider went wherever the wind would take it. Another was that a glider often slipped to one side and fell. They knew that Otto Lilienthal kept from falling by swinging his body to and fro under the wings.

Interesting as gliders were, the Wright brothers did not think that people would ever learn to fly in this way. The only answer, they believed, was a machine with an engine.

The two young men did not find the answer at once. Instead they continued to experiment with gliders that were more like Orville's box kites than like Lilienthal's leaf. Little by little they learned more about flying.

Then they took a big step ahead. This happened one day

when Wilbur Wright was twisting a cardboard box in his hands. Suddenly he noticed that although the sides remained up and down, the ends of the top and bottom of the box were twisted in opposite directions. It occurred to him that if the wing tips of a glider could be twisted in the same manner, it would have a little more surface against the air on one side and a little less on the other. If the glider started to slip in one direction this would stop it.

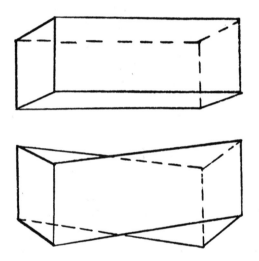

The glider the two Wrights built with this in mind had two wings with braces between them. Out in front on a spar it had a smaller plane to help it go up and down. In the rear it had a tail to steer it from side to side. All in all, it was a queer looking affair. To make it still queerer, the man who flew it had to lie flat on his stomach with his hands on the levers that worked the tail and twisted the wing tips.

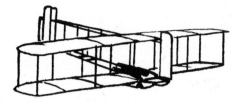

But when the Wright brothers got on a hilltop and let this glider slide down a track into the wind, it flew. They found not only that they could keep it from slipping off to one side, but also that it could be steered quite easily. This was in 1899.

While they were experimenting in this way they heard that Otto Lilienthal had been killed when his glider fell off to one side in a puff of wind. The two brothers decided to be careful and spent a long time learning to handle their machine in the air before putting an engine in it. So they went to Kitty Hawk, a quiet place in the sand dunes of North Carolina, where there were usually good winds.

Even at Kitty Hawk they could not fly every day. By 1903, after they had made some changes in the machine and learned how to warp its wings while flying, they decided to try it with an engine. On December 17 of that year their new machine ran down a track with its engine turned on. Then it leaped into the air and flew for 59 seconds without any wind to help it.

The glider had become an airplane! But the troubles of the Wright brothers were not over. Their money ran out and nobody was much interested in a flying machine. After all, most people believed it would be impossible to build one that would be practical. So the Wright brothers went back to

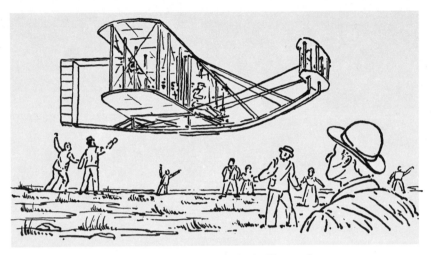

The first trial flight was made in December, 1903

Dayton and their bicycle shop, but they went right on experimenting.

By 1908 Orville Wright had succeeded in getting the army interested in the new machine, while Wilbur took one to France. And on almost the same day that Orville made a flight of over an hour at Fort Myer, Virginia, Wilbur won a valuable prize by flying for 56 minutes.

By this time several other airplane inventors had made short flights, but none of these achievements came near to equaling what the Wrights had done. It was not long before the two brothers became famous. Congress voted them a gold medal and other countries honored them in many ways. From all over the world, governments rushed to buy Wright airplanes.

In 1912, Wilbur Wright died. His brother Orville, who used to fly kites as a young man, kept on as chief engineer of his own company, and continued to invent improvements for the airplane that had made the Wright name famous.

44

3

The Cotton Gin and the Reaper

Without two machines that were invented by young Americans more than a century ago, the history of our country would probably have been quite different. Both machines made certain kinds of farming easier and more profitable.

The story of the first invention begins with the birth of Eli Whitney on a farm in Massachusetts in 1765. Even as a very small boy, Whitney was tremendously interested in tools and machines of all kinds. Because there never was much money in his home, young Eli had to work long hours on the farm. Nevertheless, he found time to study, and he saved whatever money he could get until finally he was able to go to college. He thought he would have to leave after a year, but there were so many machines around the college needing repairs and he was so very good at repairing them that he was able to pay his tuition for the full course.

During his last year at college a friend told him of a fine position as a teacher in Savannah, Georgia. Then, after he had made the long, expensive trip to Savannah, he found the post had already been given to someone else. Whitney was just about to return to Massachusetts when he met Mrs.

Greene, a widow who owned a large plantation.

Mrs. Greene's husband had been one of George Washington's most trusted generals during the War for Independence. Because he had played an important part in driving the British out of the South, the state of Georgia had given him the plantation on which Mrs. Greene now lived. Having been born in New England herself, Mrs. Greene was glad to see someone from the same part of the country, so she invited Eli Whitney to stay at the plantation for a while before going back North.

As soon as he reached the Greene plantation, Whitney began to make himself useful by repairing a churn and other broken devices. He also made several mechanical things for use around the house. This led Mrs. Greene to think that Whitney might help to solve a problem that was troubling the plantation owners. They wanted a machine that would take the seeds out of the bolls in which ripened cotton grew.

It was a very important question indeed, since the settlement of the South depended on it. Along the coast, where the land is low, the settlers could grow rice and indigo. Almost everywhere they could grow some food crops, especially corn. But there was no good way to move corn from the highlands of the interior to markets where it could be sold at a profit. The planters needed some other crop if they were to be prosperous.

About 1770 some of them tried planting cotton. At that time all the cotton in the world came from Egypt and India. Because very little of it was available, clothes made of cotton were costly and hard to get. If American soil could fill the

46

demand for cotton, this country would have a new industry that could provide a living for thousands of people.

As soon as cotton was tried in Georgia and South Carolina, the planters found that it grew better on their land than it did in Egypt or India. This was very promising, but there was a difficulty. The cotton grown in Georgia and South Carolina had short fibers and plenty of seeds. The seeds had to be combed out before the cotton could be made into thread, and because of the short fibers this work was very slow. A man working hard all day could clean only one pound of cotton. This made American cotton even more expensive than cotton from Egypt or India.

These facts were told to Eli Whitney by a planter who was a friend of Mrs. Greene's. The young man who had wanted to be a teacher looked over the cotton fields and watched workers patiently combing the seeds from the fibers. He realized at once that what was needed was a kind of comb that would work steadily instead of merely moving back and forth. To do this, the comb would have to be a round one that could be worked by a crank. The device would be still better if two combs could be made to work together.

When Whitney had gone this far, he began to build a model of the machine he had imagined. It was a wooden cylinder encircled by rows of long, thin spikes half an inch apart. At its end this cylinder was turned by a crank. The spikes then passed through a frame, or second comb, with the spaces where the spikes went through so narrow that the cotton seeds could not pass. The thin fibers would be carried through by the spikes.

Eli Whitney called his machine a "cotton gin"

On the first model he built Eli Whitney found that the fibers stuck to the spikes and were carried around again, so he added a brush at the bottom to take off the fibers. It took him less than three weeks to do this. He called his machine a "cotton gin" and as soon as it was tried out it was clear to everyone that this was just what had been needed. In a single day this first cotton gin cleaned 50 pounds of fibers! The man with the comb had been able to clean only one pound a day.

The wonderful machine had been working only a short time when someone stole it. Eli Whitney made another and sent the model to Washington, where he was given a patent on it. Meanwhile, he had entered into a partnership with Phineas Miller, a friend of Mrs. Greene's. Miller provided the money and Whitney the patent and they set up a factory at New Haven, Connecticut, to make cotton gins.

The two men were very successful because everyone wanted one of the machines that could clean 50 pounds of cotton in a single day. But the partners had their troubles, too. The machine was so simple that people began to copy it, and Whitney and Phineas Miller were forced to go to court frequently to defend themselves against people who had no right to make the cotton gin. Although the two men won every time, Whitney became so annoyed by these law suits that in 1798, only four years after he got his patent, he withdrew from the business.

By this time he had already become a rich man as the result of his invention. When he and Phineas Miller had opened their factory, they had decided not to sell their machines but to rent them. But the machines were so useful that state governments in the South offered them large sums of money if they would sell the cotton gins outright to people in their states. South Carolina alone gave Whitney and Miller $50,000, a very large sum of money for that time.

When Whitney gave up the cotton gin business, he did not lose interest in making machines that would do things better than they had ever been done before. At that time the United States was building its first navy, and to arm the ships the government had to order its guns from England. Eli Whitney thought this a fine opportunity to go into the gun-making business. He knew that all guns were made by hand, but that there were very few mechanics who could make a gun. So Whitney had another idea that counts as a great invention, although it is not one you can look at and hold in your hand.

If there were not many mechanics who could make a whole gun, there were a large number who could be taught to make one part of it. Whitney trained men in this way and taught each mechanic to make only one part of the gun over and over again. Other mechanics then fitted the parts together. If a part broke, a new one from the factory always fitted perfectly. This is the way most things are made today, but in Eli Whitney's time nobody had ever heard of such a procedure and people came from long distances to see his strange factory.

Whitney's cotton gin changed the South of our country. The next invention changed the whole world, for it had to do with the grains used in making bread—the world's most common food. These grains are easy to grow, but it was hard to get enough of them to supply people's needs. The trouble was that all the grain in a field of wheat or rye or barley ripens at once, and when it is ripe it stays that way for only about ten days. After this the grain begins to drop out of the ears onto the ground and is lost.

All the grain that is to be used must be cut during these ten days. A man with a scythe, working very fast, can cut only half an acre in a day. This meant that each man working on a farm where grain was growing could cut only five acres of it every year. Very little was left of the grain that can be grown on five acres after the needs of the farmer were taken care of. As a result grain was often scarce and many people went hungry.

This was the problem taken up by Cyrus H. McCormick. His father owned four farms in Virginia, together with two grist mills, two saw mills, and a blacksmith shop.

Young Cyrus McCormick was a tall, strong man who was much interested in how things were made. At the age of fifteen he was already suggesting improvements in some of the tools, and later he invented a new kind of plow. But what interested him most was a grain reaping machine made by his father.

Several other people had tried to reap grain by machinery. There was an English machine that worked quite well, with a line of scissors on a rod snapping back and forth. But it was often in need of repairs, and the scissors blades frequently broke against a rock or stick. Another disadvantage of this reaper was that it left the grain loosely thrown on the ground to be raked up. Then, too, all reaping machines were slow and hard to handle for they had to be pushed by horses.

McCormick wanted something that would prevent stones from touching the cutting edges of his machine, and that would provide a way of collecting the grain. The solution came to him when he put down clearly what he wanted, as often happens with inventors. He worked out the idea and had the family blacksmith make the parts, in 1831, when he was only 22 years old.

McCormick's reaper was a kind of two-wheeled car, with a bar carrying knives hanging down beside one of the wheels. Along the front edge of this bar was a series of metal fingers with sharp ends and slots in their sides. These kept stones

Cyrus McCormick invented the reaper in 1831

out of the way. A line of triangular knives was placed on another bar, which was connected to slide back and forth inside the first bar as the wheels of the car turned. These knives sheared off the grain against the fingers.

Behind the cutter McCormick placed a flat piece of canvas in a frame. The canvas caught the grain as it fell, and when there was enough for a sheaf the driver stopped and tied it up. This was a very simple machine compared to the big ones used today, but in McCormick's time it was a wonderful discovery. Any farmer could cut down seven acres of grain in a day with it instead of the half acre he could cut before. As McCormick went on improving his machine and adding new parts to it, he was soon building reapers that could cut 16 acres a day.

This happened just at the time when people began to settle

52

the plains on both sides of the Mississippi. The land was just right for growing wheat and McCormick's reapers made it possible for a few men to gather great crops of grain. Much of the wealth of our country came from the wheat fields which were made possible by McCormick's reaper.

After his invention became a success, Cyrus McCormick moved to Chicago and set up a factory. Like Eli Whitney, he frequently had to sue people who had used his patents. Although he was not as lucky as Whitney in winning all his cases in court, he continued to invent new parts for his reaper. His machines were always just a little bit better than the others so he sold more of them.

4

The Magic Performed with Words and Wires

In the middle of the eighteenth century there were a number of scientific discoveries and inventions, for people were becoming more aware of science and its wonders. Among the things frequently exhibited at parties was a device called a Leyden jar. This was a heavy glass jar partly filled with water and coated on the outside with tinfoil or some other metal. A rod extended through the top of the jar and ended in a knob. When anyone touched the outside of a jar and the knob at the same time, there was a spark and an electric shock was felt. This discharged the Leyden jar, which had to be reloaded by being connected with a machine that made electricity.

Leyden jars were curiosities of not much use except to amuse people, for the amount of electricity they stored was small. But there was one man who became deeply interested in the Leyden jar as soon as he saw it. This was Dr. Benjamin Franklin of Philadelphia.

In addition to editing a newspaper and being clerk of the General Assembly, Benjamin Franklin had already made several useful inventions. He had learned almost everything there was to learn about science at that time. Many great inventors, like Galileo Galilei and James Watt, have done more than one thing, but Franklin went beyond them all.

The first thing Franklin did with a Leyden jar was to improve it. He did not know what electricity was, but he did know that it could be sent through a metal wire. So it seemed to him that a Leyden jar would work better if it were coated both inside and out with metal instead of being partly filled with water. This turned out to be true.

Then Franklin thought that if a glass coated on both sides with metal would hold a charge of electricity, there was no special reason why it had to be in the shape of a round jar. So he took several large panes of glass, coated them on both sides with metal, connected them with wires, and ran electricity into them. He found he had been perfectly right. His panes of glass would hold far more electricity than a Leyden jar. The first electric battery had been invented.

Now Franklin became interested in putting electricity to work. He used sparks from Leyden jars to fire guns. He found that if he used very heavy jars with plenty of electricity, the shock would kill a small animal.

Being a friendly man, Franklin thought he would use this experiment to amuse his friends, so two days before Christmas in 1750 he invited a group of people in for dinner. He intended to kill the turkey for dinner by the shock from two large Leyden jars, but he began to talk to someone and, without thinking, touched the jars. The shock was enough to knock him to the floor. At the same time there was a loud bang and a big spark.

When Benjamin Franklin recovered he got to thinking that

The shock knocked Benjamin Franklin to the floor

his experience had been very much like what happened when lightning struck, though on a smaller scale. If this were true, then a wire standing upright on a roof and running down to the ground would carry away a stroke of lightning so that it would not damage the house. Franklin wrote letters to several friends suggesting this and tried it on his own house.

It worked out just as he said and lightning rods were Franklin's second electrical invention.

Now he was almost sure that even if he did not know what electricity was, he knew how it worked. Instead of being a kind of fire, as most people thought, electricity was more like a fluid. It could run out of something like a Leyden jar, along a wire, and into something else. Franklin believed, too, that lightning must be a kind of electricity. But so far this was only an idea and no use could be made of it until it was proved.

So Franklin thought of a way to prove his theory. He went out in a thunderstorm to fly a kite in which there was an iron wire to catch the lightning. As he did not want a very heavy charge, he made his kite string of twine, for twine will carry electricity but not very well. At the end of his kite string he placed a silk ribbon, which will not carry electricity at all, and between the kite string and ribbon he placed a key. When the kite was flown into a thunderstorm Franklin touched the key. This made a circuit from the top of the kite through his body into the ground. There was a spark and a small electric shock of the same kind he got from a Leyden jar.

This proved that all electricity was the same and that it flowed from one place to another, as Franklin had thought. Once this was done it became possible to make a number of electrical inventions.

Benjamin Franklin never tried to get any money for his inventions. He was glad to let people have them. Later, he helped write our Constitution and became one of the most famous men in American history. His name will come up again in this book.

In the years following Benjamin Franklin's discovery many people thought of using electricity to send messages. Several machines for this purpose were built in England, France, and Germany. Usually they caused a needle to move on a dial, pointing to one letter after another. But they all had two troubles. They worked very slowly and they could take a message only a short distance because the current leaked out the sides of the wire and became so weak that it would no longer move the needles.

In 1832 a man named Charles Jackson, who had been studying electricity in France, began talking about this to a friend during the long sea voyage from Europe to America. This friend was Samuel F. B. Morse.

Samuel Finley Breese Morse had been born in Charlestown, Massachusetts, where he grew up as a tall, strong, handsome boy. Morse was such a good student that he entered Yale College at the age of 14. There he took several scientific courses, including one in electricity, but his greatest interest was painting.

As soon as he was graduated he began to study art under a man named Alston, who took him to London. There Morse studied under Benjamin West, who had also taught Robert Fulton. When he returned to America he opened a studio in Boston as a portrait painter and became very successful. In 1823 Morse went to New York and again did well as a painter.

In the six years that followed, Samuel Morse saved up enough money to take his wife and children on a three-year trip to France and Italy, where he did more studying. He was 41 years old when he met Charles Jackson on the ship coming back. Jackson told him of Benjamin Franklin's belief that electricity would go through any length of wire. What is more, it would move so fast that its speed could not be measured!

Morse said that if electricity could be found in any part of a long wire he firmly believed it could be used to send messages. Then he began to work out a way to do it. It seemed to him that the methods already tried had two difficulties. First, it was very easy to get things wrong with pointers working on a dial. Secondly, it took quite a lot of electricity to move the pointers.

So while still on the ship, Morse worked out an alphabet of dots and dashes which could be printed or sounded on a buzzer by opening or closing an electric circuit. This is the alphabet still used in telegraph systems. On the ship he also made drawings of two different kinds of telegraph machines. When he got back to New York he almost forgot about painting to work on his idea. His two brothers gave him a room to work in and for years he did nothing but experiment with telegraphs.

We do not know when he hit on the solution of the main difficulty that had troubled the others. But sometime between 1832 and 1837 he thought up the idea of what is called a relay. This was an electric battery on the line which would add to the current every time an impulse came along the wire.

Morse experimented on his telegraph for years

Morse applied for a patent on his telegraph, formed a partnership with a Congressman, and asked Congress for money to build a line. This was needed because it was so very expensive to set up long lines of wire. Furthermore, if the telegraph worked it would be of great help to our country. But Congress was not interested, so Samuel Morse went to Europe in 1838, thinking that because there had been more experiments there, he would stand a better chance. This did not work out well. France was the only country that would give him a patent, but it was of no use to him, because a French law stated that only the government could own telegraph lines.

After eleven months Morse returned to New York. All his money was gone, he had lost most of his skill as a painter, and nobody believed in his invention. During the next four years he taught art, but made barely enough to live on. His prospects brightened when in 1842 Congress finally passed a bill allowing $30,000 for building a telegraph line.

With this money, Morse found he had solved only half his difficulties. The experimenters in Europe had buried their wires in the ground and this worked very well on the short lines they used. But when Morse tried to do this with his long line, the electricity leaked out into the ground and the line would not work at all.

A mechanic from New York named Ezra Cornell finally suggested that instead of burying the wires they should be strung on poles. The plan was successful, and on May 24, 1844, the telegraph line from Washington to Baltimore was opened. The first message, which was sent by Morse himself, was: "What hath God wrought." Next came a series of messages telling people in Washington about the results of a political convention being held in Baltimore.

It was clear at once that Morse's telegraph was faster and more reliable than any that had ever been built. Telegraph lines began to go up all over this country and Europe and Morse received many honors from foreign governments.

Although he also received a great deal of money for the use of his patents, success brought difficulties as well. Morse's invention was so simple that almost anyone could build his kind of telegraph. In fact, a number of people did so and Morse had to sue them for using his patents. In addition, the Congressman who had been his partner but who had never done anything for the telegraph sued Morse. There were years of court cases which ended only when the Supreme Court decided everything in the inventor's favor.

After this Morse bought a fine home overlooking the Hudson, and to this house visitors came from all over the world. But his inventing days were not over. On another trip to Europe Morse met the inventors of photography. This interested him as a new way of making portraits. When he returned to this country, he took the first photographs ever made in America. He lived to be over 80 years old and did a good deal of work on the submarine cable so that messages could be telegraphed across the ocean.

In 1870, a year before Morse died, a tall, thin young man of 23 came to talk with him about electricity. The young man, whose name was Alexander Graham Bell, had come to this country from Scotland to do work for deaf people. His father had invented something called "Visible Speech," which would help deaf persons to pronounce words they could not hear.

Alexander Graham Bell himself began as a student and then a teacher of elocution and became interested in the way sounds are made in people's mouths. He had invented a way for writing sounds so that anybody seeing them on paper could pronounce them. While he was doing this it occurred to him that the sounds written down in a row of signs were not so very different from the dots and dashes of Morse's telegraph. This being so, there ought to be some way to send them from place to place by electricity. That was why he came to see Morse.

After the visit Alexander Graham Bell went to Boston, to instruct teachers of the deaf. During this time he studied electricity and worked on a machine called the "phonautograph." This was intended to teach deaf people how to pronounce words. When they spoke into the machine it made a record in the form of a wavy line. Someone would then pronounce the words correctly and the deaf person could look at the two wavy lines together to see where he had made mistakes.

The phonautograph was never much of a success, but while he was working on it Alexander Graham Bell found he had to have a way of making sounds into electrical impulses. He read of experiments of this kind made more than ten years before by a German scientist named Philipp Reis.

Reis knew that sounds will cause a thin membrane to move back and forth, or vibrate. He then made these vibrations open and close an electrical circuit. This would send spoken sounds along a wire, but it was no real improvement on Morse's telegraph, because no one could understand the sounds at the other end of the wire. Every time the circuit was broken part of the sound would be lost.

But what Alexander Graham Bell needed for his phonautograph was something that would make every sound exactly right and not lose any of them. So he thought of keeping

64

Alexander Graham Bell invented the telephone in 1876

the circuit open so that the electric current would go through the wire all the time. For this to work well the amount of electricity moving through the wire would have to change as the sound changed. A membrane at the other end of the line would then vibrate in the same way as the one that was spoken to. In other words, the person who was at the receiving membrane at the end of the line would hear the sounds that were spoken into the membrane at the sending end of the line.

When Bell got this far he suddenly realized that he had something which would be of a great deal more use than merely teaching deaf people to speak correctly. He had an invention that would enable people to talk to each other over long distances. He began experimenting along this line, and succeeded in building two or three machines that worked fairly well. Then one day he said into his instrument: "Come in here, will you?" A few seconds later his assistant walked in from a distant room where he also had an instrument. The assistant had heard the message. Alexander Graham Bell had invented the telephone.

This was in 1876. In the history of great inventions no other one was ever taken up so quickly and by so many people as the telephone. Within a few years there were telephones all over the world, and Alexander Graham Bell was a great success. Nevertheless, remembering the dream that had brought him to this country, he used most of the money he earned to aid people who were deaf. When the government gave him a large prize for his invention he spent it all on setting up a laboratory to help the deaf.

Bell also found time to invent other things. He bought a large estate in Nova Scotia and experimented with breeding sheep. Later he became interested in airplanes and founded the association which arranged for the first public flights made by the Wright brothers. Later still he invented a method for keeping airplanes steady in the air and a queer-looking cigar-shaped motorboat that would go tremendously fast.

The next great inventor in the field of sending information from place to place was born just about the time Alexander Graham Bell began the experiments that led to the telephone. He was a small Italian with a round head and big ears named

The Magic Performed with Words and Wires

Guglielmo Marconi. As his father was a wealthy man, young Guglielmo was given the best of private teachers and allowed to study anything he wanted. He selected electricity as his favorite subject. So it happened that at an age when most boys are still in high school, Guglielmo Marconi was writing to scientists all over Europe about electricity and reading reports of their experiments.

Among the papers he read, Marconi came upon the news of experiments made by a German scientist named Heinrich Hertz. Hertz was a college teacher, who liked to talk and think about scientific causes, but he was not much interested in putting his theories to work. Then one day he had a dispute with some other scientists. They said that although it could be proved by mathematics that electrical waves travel through the air, no one could really find the waves. This annoyed Hertz, so he went to work on the problem and after several years of experimenting, he succeeded in proving his point.

He did this by making an electric spark jump across a gap and showed that when this happens, an electric current is set up in a wire at some distance from the spark. Then Hertz lost interest. Guglielmo Marconi and many others thought that if a spark could give off electrical waves and could be made to produce a current at a distance, it could be used for sending messages. The trouble was that when experimenters tried to put their theory into action, the current at the opposite end from the spark was so weak it was of no use.

Trying to solve this difficulty, Marconi hunted through

everything that had been written about electricity, and finally came across something that he thought might help.

An experimenter named D. E. Hughes in England had found out that when an electric spark was set off near a tube packed with iron filings, the filings would let a greater amount of electrical current run through them. Hughes, like Hertz, had not tried to do anything with this. It was just an interesting scientific fact, one of the things experimenters find out when they try things to see what will happen. Hughes had not even thought it worth while to write it down at first.

Marconi built a tube full of iron filings and set a current running through it. Then he let off an electric spark near by to increase the amount of current going through the iron filings. No matter how small the increase was, the fact that there was more current than before could be made to work some kind of key or buzzer.

So in 1895, when he was only 21 years old, Guglielmo Marconi began experimenting with this device on his father's estate in northern Italy. He had a sending circuit with a key that could open or close the circuit. When the key was closed an electric spark jumped down a line of metal balls. At the other end he placed his tube of filings, and the current running through it drove a buzzer. With this first wireless Marconi found he could send messages for more than a mile. This meant that it would work if he could make enough improvements in the details.

So Marconi went to work. First he changed the iron filings in his tube, or "condenser" as he called it, for a mixture of

In 1895 Marconi experimented with the first wireless

nickel and silver, which will carry much more electricity than
iron. Then he attached this sending circuit to a metal plate
buried in the ground. Finally he mounted the wires on tall
towers to keep clear of things that might be in the way. It
took nearly two years to work out the details and get the invention patented. Within a year after he received his patent,
Marconi was talking to ships of the Italian navy twelve miles
at sea.

Compared to many inventors Marconi had an easy time
getting people to accept what he had made. But he kept right
on working and added many other inventions to his original
wireless. In 1910 he found out how to send a wireless beam
in only one direction. During the first World War he worked
for the Italian army and navy and discovered how to send
messages for very long distances. He was honored by many
governments and became recognized as one of the world's
greatest scientists.

Improvements in sending messages had moved much more
rapidly than improvements in writing and printing. It was a
long time after Gutenberg before anyone else thought of
something that would help people to communicate better by
the written word. Like many other inventions this one had
to wait for something else to be invented first.

From the time James Watt invented the steam engine and
Eli Whitney the cotton gin, people kept trying to do things
by machinery that they used to do by hand, but it was not
always easy. One of the things a great many inventors tried
was to find a way of writing letters by machine instead of

by hand. Several such machines were patented after 1800, but they were all too slow to be of any real use.

The man who made the first practical typewriter was Christopher Latham Sholes. He was a newspaper editor in Milwaukee, Wisconsin, who loved to play chess and read poetry, and who cared so little for money that he was nearly always in need of it. In addition to his other hobbies he liked to tinker with mechanical ways of doing things. He worked out a method for getting newspapers to the subscribers by printing their names on the margin of the paper.

In 1860, Christopher Sholes was editor of the Milwaukee *Sentinel*. His paper supported Abraham Lincoln for President in the election that year and when Lincoln was elected he rewarded Sholes by appointing him Collector of Customs for the port of Milwaukee. This gave Sholes enough to live on and the work was easy, so he had plenty of time to tinker with inventions. Since he was a newspaper man most of these inventions had something to do with printing.

In 1864 Sholes and a friend worked out a machine for numbering the pages of books and built the model in a small machine shop. The owner of the machine shop told Sholes about a writing machine of which he had seen a model. It had letters around a cylinder. When a key was pressed the cylinder turned and a small hammer drove the paper against the proper letter. Nearly all the writing machines made so far worked in this way.

Sholes saw how useful a machine that would write in type would be, but he thought this a very clumsy way to do it. From then on, he spent all his time in working out a better

Christopher Sholes' typewriter as it looked in use

one. He wanted something that would not have so many parts and would work faster and more easily. It took him nearly three years trying different ways of doing what he wanted to do.

One day when he was visiting a friend in a telegraph office, he saw a telegraph key being pressed down with its upper arm closing the circuit, and this gave him the idea he needed. If there were a hinge to the key and the upper arm carried a letter it could be made to strike against a piece of paper. And if there were a number of keys, each with one letter, the turning cylinder would not be needed. He made a model with only one key carrying the letter "w" and it worked. This was the first typewriter.

A year later, in 1868, Sholes received his patent on a writing machine that had all the letters of the alphabet. He needed money so badly that he sold all his rights to the Remington Company, which up to that time had made nothing but guns. When Sholes got to be an old man he said that he had spent all his life trying to escape being a millionaire and he thought he had succeeded.

About the time Sholes' new typewriter was coming into use the model of another kind of writing machine was brought to a clever young mechanic in Baltimore named Ottmar Mergenthaler. He was from Germany, where all the members of his family were teachers. Ottmar Mergenthaler was supposed to become a teacher too, but when he was fourteen he said he wanted to be a mechanic instead, so he was apprenticed to a maker of watches and clocks. He showed so much skill that after four years a friend of the family who had a business in Washington asked him to go there and work.

The business was one of making scientific instruments. Ottmar Mergenthaler not only enjoyed himself but quickly showed that he was very good at the work. Many inventors went to Washington to get patents, and as they were required to have models of their inventions, a number of them had the models made by the young German mechanic. In this way he got to know not only the inventors, but a good deal about mechanical things as well.

In 1876 the young man's employer moved to Baltimore and Ottmar Mergenthaler went with him. It was there that the model of a new kind of writing machine was brought to him. This machine did not work very well, and the inventor wanted Mergenthaler to improve it.

Mergenthaler worked on it for a time and succeeded in making valuable changes. Still it was not as good as Sholes' typewriter and nothing came of it. But it gave Mergenthaler an idea for solving a problem that had bothered printers ever since Gutenberg.

This was the fact that in printing, someone had to pick up the separate type letters one by one, and arrange them. Then, when the printing job was done, the letters had to be put away again.

It seemed to Mergenthaler that there ought to be a way of pressing a key and having the right type drop out of a box. It was easy to think up a machine that would do this, and some had already been built, but for two reasons none was very useful. They could not put the type away after the printing had been done and someone still had to put in blank spaces of the right width to make each line the right length.

The idea that occurred to Mergenthaler was that things would be much easier if the type did not have to be put away after printing. In other words, would it not be possible to cast a whole line of type in one solid block? This would be much easier to handle than single letters. Although Mergenthaler was a very clever mechanic, it took him nearly seven years to work out the details of a machine that would do what he wanted.

Mergenthaler's linotype machine

He solved the question of the spaces by making them in the shape of wedges which could be inserted into a line of type and would always be just as wide as needed. When he had finished, Ottmar Mergenthaler had invented the linotype machine with which most typesetting is done today.

5

Inventions for the Home

If you compare your home with the home of one hundred years ago, you will have some understanding of what inventors have done to make life simpler and more pleasant. Two great inventions for the home were the work of men about whom we know very little. The first was Bartolomeo Cristofori, who lived in Padua in northern Italy. The only other detail known about this man was that he made musical instruments called harpsichords.

At that time, about 1700, Italy was split up into many small states ruled by princes. Prince Ferdinand, the ruler of Florence, was fond of music and had a fine collection of musical instruments. Needing someone to keep his instruments in good repair, he sent for Bartolomeo Cristofori and gave him a post at the court. Among the instruments in Prince Ferdinand's collection were not only harpsichords but also dulcimers.

A harpsichord is an instrument with keys like the keys of a piano. When harpsichord keys are struck, they pluck at strings, thus making sounds. The harpsichord has a sweet tone, but it cannot be played very fast and is never very loud.

A dulcimer looks like a box with strings across it. The

Cristofori called his invention a "pianoforte"

player holds it on his lap and strikes the dulcimer strings with little padded hammers. It can be played quite fast and the strings will give off a lot of sound. The player of a dulcimer must be skillful enough to avoid striking more than two notes at once.

As Bartolomeo Cristofori repaired the Prince's instruments, the idea came to him that if he could arrange a dulcimer so that it could be played with keys like those of a harpsichord, he would have an instrument that would be better than either of the other two. It was not hard to think of fitting a key and hammer to each string. The difficulty was of another kind. If the hammers came down to strike the strings and then rested on them, there would be no music, for the strings would not vibrate.

78

Cristofori must have worked on this problem for some time. Finally he solved it by having the hammers come up from underneath to strike the strings and then fall back by themselves. There were several other clever ways of doing things in what Cristofori called his "pianoforte," from two Italian words which mean soft and loud.

When he was done he had invented the most useful musical instrument in history. But the piano has a strange story. People in Italy did not like it, so the pianos Cristofori built were stored away in collections or allowed to fall to pieces. Nothing more might have been heard of them but for a poet at the court of the King of Saxony. This man came upon an essay about Cristofori's piano and was so interested that he translated it into German.

At this same court, the King of Saxony's musical instruments were taken care of by a man named Gottfried Silbermann. When he read about Cristofori's pianos, Silbermann became excited over the idea of the new instruments and built several of them. German musicians liked them, and soon everyone was playing the piano. But by that time Bartolomeo Cristofori was dead.

The story of James Hargreaves begins like that of Cristofori. It is not known when Hargreaves was born, where he went to school, or whether he went to school at all. The first thing we hear of him is that he was a carpenter and weaver at Blackburn in northern England in 1760. There he was hired by a rich man to build a device to "card" or straighten out the fibers of wool.

The first spinning jenny was built about 1764

At this time most people had to spin their own thread, using the spinning wheels you sometimes see in pictures. One day at James Hargreaves' home the spinning wheel fell over on its side while it was working. Both the wheel and the spindle on which the newly made thread was wound kept on turning. The spindle on a spinning wheel lies flat, so when this one was turned on its side it came into an upright position.

It occurred to James Hargreaves that if the spindle were placed on its end like this, it would be possible to use more than one and so spin several threads at a time. He built a machine that would do this with a frame to draw out and twist the threads. This was the first spinning jenny, built about 1764, and named for Hargreaves' daughter Jenny.

At first the inventor used his machine only to make thread for his own weaving, but he had a large family to support, so he built several other jennies and sold them. From the very beginning the machines made thread five or six times as fast as it could be spun by hand. Later, Hargreaves made better ones that worked even faster, but this began to anger his neighbors. Nearly everyone who lived near by was in the weaving or spinning business. People who worked at the old-fashioned wheels became afraid that the new invention would put them out of work. In 1768 a mob of spinners gathered around Hargreaves' house, threw all his furniture outdoors, and burned his jenny and loom.

After this Hargreaves moved his family to Nottingham, where he interested a Mr. James in the new machine. The two men went into partnership and set up a cotton mill in which the spinning was done by Hargreaves' jennies. The mill was very profitable, but Hargreaves did not patent his great invention until 1770. By that time a number of manufacturers were using copies of the jennies which Hargreaves had built. Although he sued these people, it was proved that he had sold his machines without having a patent, so he got nothing at all.

James Hargreaves' spinning jenny made it possible to turn out large quantities of cloth with very little work. After the machines came into use, people could afford more clothes than ever before. Six years after Hargreaves died in 1778, there were 20,000 of his jennies being used in England.

The Franklin stove became very popular

The next great invention for use in homes brings us back to Benjamin Franklin. In his time people did all their cooking in fireplaces, which meant that everything had to be boiled in a kettle or roasted on a slowly turning spit. Stoves made of tiles were used in Germany and Holland but they were for heating rooms, rather than for cooking.

Benjamin Franklin did not like the German and Dutch stoves because he was unable to see the fire. But fireplaces used a great deal of wood without heating rooms the way he wanted them heated. So in 1742 he invented a way of making better use of his fuel. Franklin's invention was a cast-iron fireplace that was set inside the brick fireplace. The smoke went up the back and there was a flat top and a piece across the front above the fire.

This device was called the Franklin stove. It became very popular at once because it gave off so much more heat than a fireplace for the same amount of fuel. After people began to use the stoves, it occurred to a number of persons at once that the front could be completely covered. If this were done, the stove could be placed out in the room away from the fireplace. It would then be possible to cook on top of the stove.

No one person invented all the details of the modern kitchen stove. As with many inventions it grew up step by step. At first stoves were heated by wood and coal, but later gas and electricity were used. The stove has gone through many changes, but it started when Benjamin Franklin decided he wanted his rooms heated better than a fireplace could do it. Franklin never took any money for this invention. He said he was glad that his stove had made it possible for people to save money on fuel.

Probably few machines have made work easier for more people than the sewing machine. It has a peculiar history. People began thinking about sewing machines almost as soon as they began thinking about machines, because sewing is so hard to do by hand. Several inventors made machines that would sew in a way, and one of them named Walter Hunt thought of the idea of using a curved needle with the eye in its point. When this was run through the cloth it would leave a little loop of thread, and the next time the needle came through the cloth, it would pass through the loop and make another loop at the same time.

The trouble with this machine was that it made what is

called a "chain stitch." It holds the cloth together, but if just one thread breaks and is pulled the whole seam comes out. A young mechanic named Elias Howe was working in a machine-shop in Cambridge, Massachusetts, when he got one of these machines to repair. It seemed to him that this was a poor way to make a sewing machine, so he began working on one that used two threads. When the curved needle came through the cloth and made its loop, a little bobbin underneath the cloth ran through the loop with this second thread and fastened it.

This was an important invention, but Elias Howe found that no one in America was interested in his machine, so he took it to England. There a man who made corsets paid him a small amount for the English patent and hired him to make the machines work. Howe stayed in England for four years. When he came back to America he found that several people considered his machine so good that they were selling copies of it, since it was not patented in America. Howe sued them all in the lawcourts and won every case, so that he became more than a millionaire. To the end of his life he kept building small machines, some of them very queer ones for which nobody could figure out any use.

Perhaps the man who did most to make everyday life what it is today was Thomas A. Edison. When Edison was quite a small boy he decided that he was going to invent things. Before he was ten years old he gave one of his friends some fizz powder in water in the hope that it would make him light enough to fly! When he was twelve he sold newspapers on a train. During his free time on the train, he read scientific books and experimented in a chemical laboratory he had set up in the corner of a railroad car. The money from his newspapers paid for the chemicals. Later he set up a telegraph line to the house of a friend and practiced telegraphy so well that by the time he was sixteen he obtained a position as a telegrapher on the railroad.

He was a strange man who gradually became deaf but never needed much sleep. After working all day he would sit up till four in the morning studying electrical science. His first invention was one for killing cockroaches by electricity in the Boston telegraph office. Not long after that, he invented a machine for telling brokers the prices of stocks on the New York Stock Exchange. This brought him so much money that at the age of 23 he was able to retire from other work and do nothing but invent.

He set up a laboratory at Menlo Park in New Jersey, got mechanics and chemists to help him, and began inventing. In six years he had patents on 122 inventions. At one time he was working on 45 different inventions at once. Other inventors came to him for help, and Edison had a good deal to do with making the Sholes typewriter practical. He invented the mimeograph. He invented wax paper for wrapping food. He invented the modern system of fire alarms. He invented a way of sending several different telegraph messages over the same line. He made improvements in Alexander Graham Bell's telephone.

In fact it is hard to do anything without running into one of Edison's inventions. His first really great one came in 1877 as the result of some work he was doing on the telephone. At the back of the telephone instrument with which Edison was working, there was a fine steel point. When he spoke into the instrument, the vibration made by his voice caused the point to prick his finger.

Now all scientists knew that sound causes vibrations in anything small enough to be moved, but no one had thought of using this knowledge. Edison had the idea that if these vibrations would drive a needle, they could be made to drive the needle into something and leave a mark. He believed that another needle passing over the same mark would cause the same sound to be repeated.

So he tried saying "Hello" into the telephone while he passed a piece of heavy telegraph paper across the needle. When he passed the paper back a second time the needle followed the marks it had made and the telephone said "Hello" very faintly but quite clearly.

This is how great inventions often begin. The inventor notices that something queer happens when he puts things together and then tries to think of a way of using what has happened. An idea usually comes easily, but after the first step the inventor has to think of a way of making his idea practical. That is very much harder. In this case Edison worked a long time on the details.

His first machine had a copper cylinder turned by hand and covered with tinfoil, in which a rather dull needle cut patterns as someone spoke into a horn to make the needle vibrate. It was not a very good machine but word soon spread that Edison had invented a device that would talk. Thousands

Edison called his talking machine a "phonograph"

of people came to hear it, and he even traveled to England to show it there.

By the time he got a patent on his talking machine, he was already making improvements on it, and he kept right on making them after people began to buy the new "phonographs." Exhibiting the machine took up so much of Edison's time that he had to lay aside another idea he had been working on since 1876. This was the invention of an electric light that would work.

Edison began on this by trying to use in electric batteries strips of paper which had been held in an oven until they became a kind of charcoal. While he was doing this he noticed that when an electric current was passed through a strip of such paper it would heat up until the paper became red and then almost white.

The inventor was sure that what he had noticed could be used to produce light from electricity, but there was a difficulty. As soon as the charred paper, or carbon, became white hot it burned because of the contact with the oxygen in the air. To keep the carbon from being touched by air, Edison first pumped the air out of a jar that was partly made of glass. Then he sent the current through a piece of carbon that had been placed inside the jar. The carbon did not last much longer than it had in the open air.

This was as far as he had gone when the phonograph made him lay aside the electric light for several months. After that he took a vacation in the West, the first one he had ever taken in his life. While he was away, he began to think out some of the problems an electric light would bring. He was sure he could make a practical light, but the experiments would be expensive, and after the light was made there would have to be some way of getting electricity to people.

When he returned from his vacation Edison hit upon a solution to his problems. He persuaded some rich men to organize an electric light company to pay for the experiments. The men wanted to know how they were going to get their money back, so Edison invented a system of central electric stations and the meter that would measure the amount of electricity used. All this was done before he had invented the light itself!

Then he went to work on the light again, although a committee of scientists in England had just voted that such a light

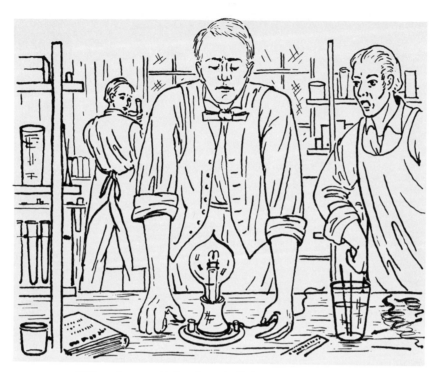

Edison invented the electric light in October, 1879

was impossible. Edison had to set up his own glass shop and work in it himself in order to get the kind of glass bulb he wanted. He found that platinum was the best material for the filament, or wire, that gives off the light inside the bulb. But platinum is a very rare and expensive metal, and he could not prevent the electric current from leaking away from the wire.

For more than a year Edison tried various other kinds of filaments. Then, one day as he sat thinking in his laboratory, he rolled in his fingers some lampblack mixed with tar which he had been using in a new type of telephone. When he looked down, he saw that he had made a kind of thread. At once the right idea came to him.

What he really wanted was a thread of carbon. He sent one of his assistants out for some ordinary sewing thread. This was baked in an oven, but most of the thread broke before it could be placed in a glass globe. Only one small piece remained, and Edison put it into a bulb. When the current was turned on, the bulb lit up and stayed lighted for more than 40 hours, beginning on October 21, 1879.

This was the first electric light. But the problem was not completely solved. It would not be practical to use a whole spool of thread for every light. Furthermore, a light that lasted only 40 hours was not good enough, so a search began for material from which to make filaments.

Edison also helped to develop motion pictures

Edison's assistants went all over the world looking for types of fibers that might be used. Japanese bamboo made fairly good ones, but it was not until seven years later that Edison himself invented an artificial fiber that would do. This shows how much work must often go into an invention before it is ready for everyday use.

While Edison was trying to get the right kind of thread for use in his light, he also invented an electric locomotive for trains. Then he looked about for something else to invent, so he got in touch with George Eastman of Rochester. Eastman had just invented a method of taking pictures on celluloid film in rolls. It seemed to Edison that this way of taking pictures could be used to make pictures that would seem to move on a screen. It did not take him long to find a practical way of making movies.

Edison lived to be over 84 years old and was granted patents on more than a thousand inventions. He was one of the greatest inventors who ever lived.

6

Steel and the Skyscraper

Many times in this book we have met inventors who were interested in almost everything. You are about to meet another such man—Henry Bessemer. During his life Bessemer invented many things, most of which were useful.

Henry Bessemer's father had a shop at Charlton near London where he made gold chains and type for printing. The son, too, liked to work with his hands, and making models of things became his hobby.

After young Henry began to study engineering, his father bought him a small lathe and other tools with which the boy could make articles of metal.

When he was 17 he went to London and set up his own shop. The more things he made, the more he thought of better ways of making things. He invented a new way of stamping official papers and a new kind of pencil. He invented a new kind of gold paint and by 1840, when he was 27, he had already made a good deal from his invention.

At that time he became interested in building, for the British navy, guns that would shoot farther and hit harder He thought at first that this could be done by changing the shape of the guns or the way they were made. But as soon as he went to places where guns were tested, he found that the real cause of the trouble was the iron of which most guns were made. It was so brittle that the guns burst when large powder charges were used in them.

We now know that this was because the cast iron of which the guns were made contained too much carbon. Coal is a form of carbon. The carbon got into the iron when the iron ore was being melted down in furnaces, where coal was mixed with it to give the heat. In Henry Bessemer's time all this had not been discovered. But Bessemer did know that when a small amount of iron was cast into the blocks called pigs there would be on top a thin layer of the better iron called steel. This was cut off the pig and sold separately.

Steel is much tougher than ordinary cast iron and in addition it can be rolled or hammered into various shapes when it is hot. Therefore it was in great demand, but because there was so little steel, it was very expensive and things made of it were rare.

Later the iron makers discovered how to make small amounts of steel by melting iron in little pots called crucibles and skimming off the impurities on top. But this was still so costly that steel could be used only in very small articles. Henry Bessemer was aware of these facts, but he thought that if he could find a way of making steel more easily he could produce the guns he wanted. He now had enough money to set up a small iron works at a place named St. Pancras, and there he began to experiment.

He asked himself what made iron change to steel. Nobody

Bessemer invented a converter that changed iron into steel

knew, but it seemed to Henry Bessemer that it might have something to do with the fact that while the iron ore was being melted a stream of air was blown over it to make the fire burn faster. He was right about this, of course. We now know that the stream of air helped to burn and carry away the carbon. As a result, the iron on top changed to steel Henry Bessemer decided to work on his theory by blowing a stream of air through the melted iron in a furnace to see what would happen.

What happened was that steel was produced! After Bessemer had his method patented, he described the process to a gathering of scientists and engineers who met in 1856. Many of those present did not believe him, so he invited them to visit him at his small factory and he made steel while they watched.

All the iron makers of the country became interested and five different companies agreed to pay for the use of his patents. This was agreeable to Henry Bessemer, who wanted to go on inventing other things without bothering with steel. But soon he began to get complaints. Although the five companies did just as he told them, their iron would not turn to steel, or even to the halfway stage which is known as malleable iron.

This was discouraging, but Bessemer dropped other things and began experimenting again to see what had gone wrong. He worked for more than two years, changing the shape of his blowers and the method of blowing and adding various substances to the iron. Sometimes the result would be steel or malleable iron, but sometimes it would not. There didn't seem to be any reason for the successes or failures. One batch would turn into good steel while another one treated exactly the same way would be plain, ordinary iron.

Finally Bessemer got a letter from a Mr. Göransson in Sweden. This man had tried Bessemer's method and had made steel every time. All at once Bessemer began to see what the trouble had been. Swedish iron ore is pure and of a fine quality. But Bessemer and the manufacturers who had failed had been using a poorer quality of iron ore from South

Wales. He tried again with better ore and, like Mr. Görans-son, was immediately successful.

When Bessemer went to the manufacturers with the news that he had solved the problem of making steel, no one would believe him and no one wanted to pay for the use of his method. With some money he had earned from other inventions and with the help of his friends, Bessemer set up a factory to make steel. This was taking a big chance because the methods of getting all impurities out of the ore were not yet perfect. But Bessemer kept experimenting while his factory was making steel. Before another year had passed he was able to sell steel at less than half the price his competitors were asking.

That was the end of opposition to his methods. All the big companies hurried to buy permission to make Bessemer steel. Soon the new process spread all over the world. The Queen of England gave him the title, Sir Henry Bessemer.

One of Bessemer's later inventions was a ship in which nobody who remained in the cabin could be seasick. If the ship rocked in one direction, the cabin would swing in the opposite direction. The theory was that this procedure would keep the cabin level. In 1875 Sir Henry had such a ship built at his own expense. It was not as successful as his method of making steel, for when the ship put to sea, the people became as seasick as if they had been aboard an ordinary ship.

Sir Henry Bessemer's discovery of a process for making steel made possible our great modern cities, but our tall buildings are directly the result of the work of another inventor,

George A. Fuller. Unfortunately, Fuller became ill and died before he could see his invention put into general use.

As a young man Fuller went to work in the office of his uncle, who was an architect in Worcester, Massachusetts. George Fuller's job was to draw the plans for buildings that were about to be erected. As he worked, he became interested in the problem of how much weight the parts of a building would carry. To this end, he spent his evenings studying engineering.

Many times he told people that the designs they brought to him were not strong enough to carry the weights that would be placed on them. Because he was always able to prove his statements by means of figures, more and more people came to consult him.

When he was 25 years old a firm of architects in Boston made him a partner, but he did not stay there long. He became more and more interested in calculating weights and less and less in designing buildings. Actually, in Boston there was not much building being done at the time except for homes or small stores, where such calculations are not very important. So in the 1880s George Fuller went to Chicago. That city was growing rapidly and, as it is built on soft ground, accurate calculations were very important.

George Fuller set up a business as a contractor—one who would erect buildings designed by other architects. One architect with whom he liked to work was named D. H. Burnham. Burnham designed fine buildings and Fuller built them solidly, so the two men became a great success. Late in the 1890s both were called to New York.

Steel and the Skyscraper

This came about as the result of a theory that Fuller had discussed with architects and builders. It concerned the materials of which buildings could be constructed. Up to that time, large buildings had always been made of stone or stone and brick. But as stone and brick buildings grew taller, the columns supporting them had to be larger, while space in the lower stories had to become smaller. Taller buildings could be built, but they were either like the pyramids, of not much use for anything, or like the great cathedrals without any upper floors to add weight. Five or six stories was the usual limit for building in stone.

During the middle of the nineteenth century some builders began to use hollow iron columns along walls. This allowed the walls to be thinner and the buildings taller. Some ten-story buildings and a few even taller were built. What called George Fuller and D. H. Burnham to New York was the demand for a building that had to be much higher than ten stories to be of any use at all.

At Broadway and 23rd Street in New York City, there was a long, narrow triangle of land that would be an excellent place for an office building. Because the land was in the middle of the business district, the taxes were very high. To pay these taxes, it would be necessary for the new building to rent out a great many offices. This meant it would have to be taller than any office building ever built before.

The owners of the property thought that perhaps the method George Fuller had been talking about could be used. This involved the use of steel, which could now be bought cheaply, thanks to Bessemer's invention. George had thought

*George Fuller designed the Flatiron Building, New York City's first
skyscraper*

of a building in which all the weight would be carried by fairly thin steel beams instead of iron columns or heavy stone piers. The steel beams would be riveted together to form a cage. Other steel beams would run from one side of the cage to the other, tying the whole building together. The walls and floors would be held up by this steel cage.

This was just the opportunity George Fuller wanted. He set about designing the tallest office building ever imagined. Many people thought it would fail. They thought that strong winds would blow the walls in or make the steel cage bend so much that the whole thing would fall apart. But Fuller made his calculations and went ahead.

In 1902, two years after he died, the Flatiron Building was finished. It was 21 stories high. After that everybody began building skyscrapers and today more than half our large office and apartment buildings are built on George Fuller's steel cage system.

7

Military Inventions

Most of the inventions used in war are not really inventions at all. Usually they are nothing more than improvements on something that has already existed. That is how it was with guns. The first ones were so big that they had to be pulled by many horses. Many people must have looked at these weapons and thought how useful it would be to have a gun small enough to be carried by a man. About 1445 some of these people began to succeed in making smaller guns.

The earliest hand guns were almost as long as a man is tall, and so heavy that the muzzle end had to be supported on a tripod when they were fired. Two men were needed to handle such a gun. One held the stock under his arm while the other man fired the gun by holding a flame to a hole at the top of the gun barrel. These early hand weapons were loaded by first putting in some gunpowder. A wad was then added to keep the force of the explosion behind the bullet. Finally, the bullet itself was inserted. After all that trouble, the weapons did not really shoot very well.

Guns kept growing lighter. Sometime around the year 1500 a German whose name we do not know thought of bending the stock down so it could be held by a man against his shoulder. This was a very important invention and in 1520 it was followed by another. Gaspard Koller, a gunsmith in Vienna, thought of the idea of rifling guns by cutting grooves along the inside of the barrel. When a bullet was fired from a rifled gun, the groove set it spinning during its flight and it was much more accurate than a bullet from a gun without the grooves.

But Koller's rifles did not become popular. In the first place nobody knew much about working in hard metals and no one could make really good rifles. In the second place it was a long, hard job to ram a bullet down a rifled gun. This made loading so slow that armies preferred to use guns with smooth bores. Finally the grooves of the rifling were hard to clean of burnt powder after the gun had been fired. Because of these difficulties, only a few rifles were made and they were mostly used by hunters.

Things remained like this for nearly 250 years. Then the pioneers of America began to push into the forests of the West. At first they got most of their meat by hunting, so they had to be sure of hitting with the first shot. For their purposes the smooth guns were not accurate enough. As the pioneers did not have to worry about reloading if the first shot hit, they began to rifle their guns. Many of them were fine craftsmen and they made good rifles. It was the good shooting of American rifles more than anything else that defeated the British in the War for Independence.

But rifles were still not very popular with anyone but hunters until two more inventions were made. Long ago it

1450

1620

1750

1950

Guns through the years

had been found that an easy way to carry ammunition was to put the bullet and the necessary amount of powder together in a paper cylinder called a cartridge. When a man wished to use one he tore open the bottom of the cartridge, poured the powder into the gun, and then rammed the bullet down on it. A little of the powder ran out the touch-hole at the side of the gun into a steel pan and was fired by a flint hammer which struck the pan and made a spark. It often failed to make a spark and sometimes the spark failed to strike the powder.

This problem was solved by a Scottish clergyman named Reverend Alexander John Forsyth who was fond of hunting. Mr. Forsyth missed so many birds because his gun failed to fire that he decided to do something about it. Having a good knowledge of chemistry, he experimented with substances that would explode more easily than gunpowder. He considered placing at the bottom of the cartridge a small amount of a substance called fulminate which would explode if struck a sharp blow. A gun using this cartridge would not need a spark. Soon Mr. Forsyth's cartridge came into common use, and the pan and touch-hole were no longer needed.

This was a great improvement as it was no longer necessary to tear open each cartridge. It still did not make rifles any more popular because they were so slow to load and so hard to clean. The next step was taken by a Frenchman named Minié, who decided that the main trouble with rifles sprang from the type of bullet that was being used. When a bullet was small enough to be rammed into the rifle easily it was so small that most of the force of the exploding powder was lost around it. So Minié invented a bullet with a soft metal base. When this base expanded it filled up the grooves, keeping the explosion from escaping.

Minié's bullets were a great success from the start. Both the British and French governments paid him large sums of money and soon all the armies of the world were exchanging their smooth guns for rifles. But even with fulminate and Minié bullets that were easy to get into the gun, loading still took a long time, and rifles were hard to clean.

The right answer to this problem had been thought of by a good many people. It was to make a gun that would load from the back end, or breech, instead of ramming the cartridge down the muzzle. Making such guns was easy, and many of them had been built. The trouble was that when a gun that loaded from the breech was fired, part of the explosion always came out the back end. Many people tried different ways of sealing the breech. Still no one could make a gun that would open to let the paper cartridge in and yet be so tight that some of the explosion would not come out.

Two other Frenchmen, named Houiller and Lefaucheux, seemed to have thought of the answer about 1850. They were Paris gunmakers who made rifles for wealthy sportsmen. Afterward each accused the other of stealing his idea. They had terrible quarrels and sued each other in the courts, but nobody has ever been able to decide which man was right.

Whichever one it was, he had an idea that was similar to Minié's. The inventor—Houiller or Lefaucheux—thought of packing the powder and bullet in a metal cylinder instead of a paper one. When the gun was fired, the explosion would all take place inside the metal case and none of it could come out the breech of the gun.

This is so simple an invention that it is rather surprising that someone did not think of it before. It was immediately successful and soon all the guns in the world were breech loaders.

The invention of the metal cartridge also had another result. For a long time people had been thinking of a gun that would fire more than one shot without reloading. This was very difficult so long as paper cartridges had to be rammed down. But when the metal cartridge came out several people began to make guns that would fire several shots without reloading.

One of the most interesting of these inventors was Samuel Colt, who came from Connecticut, where his father had a silk factory. At the age of ten Samuel Colt was taken out of school and placed in the factory to learn the business. After he had been there four years, his father sent him to a boarding school. Then, deciding that he was tired of both school and the silk business, Samuel Colt ran away as a cabin boy on a clipper ship bound for India.

Aboard clippers, everybody had a good deal of time free, so many of the sailors spent their time carving ship models and other articles. Samuel Colt carved too, but the idea of making ship models did not interest him. Instead he carved out a wooden model of a gun that would fire six times without reloading. Instead of one breech it had six. After it was fired, the hammer was pulled back to bring another breech with its cartridge into line with the barrel.

Samuel Colt called his gun a revolver

When Samuel Colt returned from his runaway voyage he decided that working in the silk factory was not so bad after all. He went back to it but he spent much of his time learning chemistry in the dyeing department of the plant. He soon acquired such a good knowledge of chemistry that, although he was only 18 years old, he was able to travel across the country giving lectures on the subject.

In three years he had earned enough money to start a factory for the manufacture of his guns, which he called "revolvers." Some of these were bought by army officers who liked them very much. But this was only 1833, when cartridges were still made of paper. Not all the guns worked well, and so few people bought them that in 1842 Samuel Colt's factory failed.

In 1847 the United States went to war with Mexico. General Zachary Taylor, who later became President, commanded one of the armies. He was among the officers who had used Colt's revolver in fights with the Indians and he wanted all his soldiers to be armed with them. The United States Government hunted up Samuel Colt and gave him an order for thousands of guns. This made it easy for the inventor to borrow money and start a new factory.

Not long afterward the metal cartridge was invented and soon everybody was buying Colt's revolvers. He went on inventing, thinking up improvements for his revolvers, and machines with which to make revolver parts. Every type of machine gun dates back, in some way, to the little wooden model Samuel Colt carved during his runaway trip to India.

The great invention that changed big guns to the same extent that the metal cartridge had changed small ones was made by a man named Henri Joseph Paixhans. He grew up in the time of Napoleon and, after going to a technical school, became an officer of artillery. As Napoleon was nearly always fighting a war with somebody, Henri Joseph Paixhans soon had a great deal of experience. When peace came there was not much for an artillery officer to do, so Paixhans began to study two things—guns and politics.

At that time nearly all guns fired round balls of solid iron. There were also mortars which fired what were called bombs.

These were hollowed-out powder-filled metal balls to which fuses were attached. When a mortar was fired the explosion lighted the fuse and the fuse was supposed to set off the powder in the bomb when it struck the target. Sometimes the bomb went off before reaching the target, and sometimes the fuse failed to catch fire so that it never went off at all. Moreover, a mortar was difficult to aim, for after firing, its bomb would shoot upward and then come down at an angle.

But bombs could not be fired from cannon aimed straight at a target because they would not be in the air long enough for a long fuse to burn. If, on the other hand, the fuse were made quite short, the bomb was apt to go off in the gun. This was the problem that Colonel Paixhans took up, but before attacking it, he separated it into two problems.

He decided that his first need was a cannon that would get the bomb out of the gun so quickly that there would be no chance for accidents. This could be done if the bomb were made to fit tightly in the gun so that none of the force of the explosion was lost. Secondly, he needed a new kind of fuse, one that did not have to be lighted by the explosion.

Then it occurred to him that this was similar to the problem that the Reverend Alexander Forsyth had solved for small guns. There was one difference: this time the explosion was not wanted in the gun but in the bomb it fired. So instead of putting a cap with fulminate in his gun, he put one at the end of his bomb. This changed the shape of the bomb from round to long and narrow. When it struck something solid a hammer in it would be driven against the cap and the bomb would go off.

Paixhans' exploding shells were tried out for the

It was Colonel Paixhans' hope that his new bomb would be used by the forts which defended the coast of France against enemy navies. He claimed that if guns and bombs were made his way no wooden ship could stand up against them. Here Paixhans was fortunate. The plans of most military inventors are not tried until war occurs, but Colonel Paixhans knew how to make use of his knowledge. He persuaded his political friends that the army needed, for tests, two of his guns and a supply of bombs.

The two guns were fired at an old wooden battleship in Brest harbor. Every one of the bombs went off, tearing great holes in the ship and setting her afire. Paixhans' invention was such a great success that solid shot is no longer used. Instead, armed forces use bombs, or shells as they are now called.

Eventually Colonel Paixhans became a member of the

first time on a wooden battleship in Brest harbor

French parliament, and when he retired he was made a general. He lived to be a very old man and grew roses in his garden while people were using his guns and shells.

When Colonel Paixhans made a report on his new invention he said ships would have to put on iron armor. But nothing was done about it for nearly 30 years. At that time, mills were unable to roll thick iron plates. When engineers bolted several thin iron plates together and fired at them, the shot went right through.

Early in the 1850s a French iron maker found a means of rolling plates four inches thick. These were able to keep out the shot fired by the guns of that day, so the French built several iron-plated vessels. They had neither engines nor masts and had to be towed from place to place, so they were hardly

113

really ships. But in 1852, when France was at war with Russia, iron-plated vessels went into action against the Russian batteries at Kinburn on the Black Sea and at once showed how useful they could be. Shells from the iron-plated vessels, which were undamaged by the guns on shore, pounded the batteries to pieces.

After this the French and British navies built steam frigates with iron plates along their sides. But when the Civil War broke out in the United States, this country had done nothing about adding armored vessels to our fleet. The war had been going on for four months before Congress passed a bill allowing the government to build three armored ships.

Meanwhile, the Union Navy of wooden ships had blockaded the Confederate coast. As the Confederates had no real navy of their own, they became very much interested in building an armored ship that could drive off any number of wooden ones.

Two Confederate lieutenants named John E. Brooke and John L. Porter worked together on the problem. They decided they did not have time to build both a ship and her engines, for the Confederacy was short of materials. But the Union fleet at Norfolk Navy Yard had been burned when the war broke out and among the ships partly destroyed was the big steam frigate *Merrimack*. However, she had only burned as far as the water's edge, and when the Confederates raised her, the two lieutenants found that her engines would still work. They did not have time to build her sides up again and put iron plates on them, so they had to invent a new kind of ship.

On top of the deck that remained they built what they called a citadel, which looked like the upper part of a barn. The citadel was covered with four inches of armor and had portholes along the sides. In February, 1862, she was launched and made ready to destroy the blockading squadron.

The Union Government heard about the *Merrimack* and was very anxious to get at least one armored ship ready to meet her, but there was cause for worry. The naval board that was studying ironclads had some doubt whether the ship they had planned would be able to carry the weight the builder intended to put on her. So the builder, whose name was Bushnell, went to New York to consult the best engineer he knew. That engineer was John Ericsson, the man who had invented the screw propeller.

Ericsson calculated the weights on Bushnell's ship, and told him they were all right. While they were talking, Ericsson went to a heap of rubbish in the corner of his office and brought out a box. In the box was a model of a strange craft that looked exactly like a long shingle with a small round tower on top. Ericsson explained that this was his idea of an armored ship.

When Bushnell asked why he did not submit it, Ericsson said he wanted nothing to do with the Navy because it had not paid him for the *Princeton*. Bushnell offered to submit the model himself, but when he did so, the board was doubtful about it and placed many hard conditions on Ericsson. These did not stop him and he got his ship, the *Monitor*, ready in time to save the Union Navy. She was able to defeat the Confederate *Merrimack*, or *Virginia*, in a thrilling battle on

The Monitor, *designed by John Ericsson, was a*

March 9, 1862.

The *Monitor* alone proves how great an inventor John Ericsson was. She was a combination of over forty completely new inventions many of which are still in use today. Ericsson invented the engines that drove her and the rudders that steered her. The ventilators we use in our houses are improvements on those Ericsson designed for the *Monitor*. The elevators in which we ride up and down owe a great deal to the device Ericsson used to hoist shells up to the *Monitor's* turret. Ericsson built many other *Monitors* before the war was over and became one of the most honored men in the country.

Like John Ericsson, the inventor of the first really successful submarine came here from another country. He was John P. Holland, an Irish schoolteacher who studied engineering in his spare time. Holland had trouble with the British authorities because he had joined the Fenians, an organization that

combination of many inventions which are still in use today

was trying to win freedom for his country.

One day John Holland read in the paper about experiments with a submarine boat which submerged in New York harbor. This was one of a number of experimental submarines that had been built since Robert Fulton's time. Some had been fairly successful, though none had been good enough to be really practical. John Holland believed that if only a better submarine could be built it would destroy the British Navy, an event that would help Ireland's cause. So he sat down and drew designs for a submarine boat. It was really a very good design considering he had never done anything like that before. But John Holland's Fenian friends laughed at him, so he put the designs away.

In 1872, when he was 31 years old, John Holland decided to go to America with his mother. Arriving in Boston on a wintry day, he fell on the ice and broke his leg. He had to stay in bed for two months, but he made use of his time by working on his forgotten submarine designs. Although he was able to improve them considerably, nobody was interested.

So John Holland went back to teaching school and attending meetings of the Fenians. Four years later a Fenian who had some money agreed to furnish six thousand dollars to build an experimental boat. In 1878 the submarine was ready to be tested.

Now the trouble with all submarines built up to this time was that nobody had found a really good way of making them dive or of keeping them level under water after they had dived. When torpedoes had been let loose by submerged submarines, they had become so light that they had always rushed to the surface.

John Holland thought up a simple plan for overcoming these difficulties. When he wanted to dive he let water into tanks which he placed along the sides of the submarine. The submarine then became heavy enough to sink just beneath the surface of the water, though she was still light enough to float.

After two planes at the sides of the submarine were turned until they slanted down, the engine was started. This drove her under. Under water she was moved in the same way. When she lost weight by firing her weapons more water was let into the tanks to replace the weight, so she was always steady. When Holland wanted to come up again he blew the water out of the tanks with compressed air.

The first small submarine, only big enough for one man, did not work perfectly. But it was so encouraging that the Fenians furnished enough money to build a much larger

The first practical U. S. submarine

one that would hold three men. She was called the *Fenian Ram* and was launched in 1881. Many tests were made on this boat and it was the first really successful submarine. The United States Government became interested, but before things could go any further a young engineer who was working for John Holland took the boat out by himself one day. He handled her so badly that she was lost, although he himself succeeded in escaping.

Now John Holland had no more money and the Fenians had spent all theirs. He went back to teaching school and working on ideas to improve his boat. Meanwhile other engineers in other countries began building different kinds of submarines, and in 1893 the United States Navy advertised for designs for one. Only three inventors came forward. Two of their designs were accepted. One was by Holland. The other was by Simon Lake, a man who had an idea for a submarine that would run along the bottom of the ocean.

Tanks that could go across country and destroy machine guns

Of course the government paid for the building of these boats, but John Holland did not get much of the money. In fact, he was still a poor man when his boat, the *Plunger*, turned out to be a great success. But now things began to change for him. A group of rich men formed a company to build submarines for navies all over the world. They took John Holland into the company as chief engineer, and he turned over his patents in return for a salary and a sum of money.

This seemed like a sensible arrangement but it did not work out well. John Holland had used up all his ideas and could not think of ways to improve his submarine. As for the company, it found that foreign navies refused to buy submarines built in America; they were interested only in purchasing the right to use Holland's patents. The inventor thought he could have rented out the patents himself. After

were invented and used for the first time during World War I

a quarrel with his partners, he left the company. He died in 1914, just before submarines began to show what dangerous ships they could be.

The second great invention in World War I came about in almost as queer a way as Holland's submarine. Soon after the war broke out between Germany and the Allies in 1914, the opposing armies dug lines of trenches that stretched all the way from the English Channel to the mountains of Switzerland. These trenches were defended by barbed wire and thousands of machine guns. It was impossible to break through them for any great distance.

At this time there was in the British Army an engineer officer named Lieutenant Colonel E. D. Swinton. He had a fine imagination and had written a number of stories about wars and new inventions used in them. When he saw the

121

trenches and barbed wire in France he knew that soldiers could not force their way through such obstacles. But it seemed to him that if men could be placed in some kind of vehicle with armor that would keep out a machine gun bullet, the problem would be solved.

At this time there were some armored autos, but they could only run on roads. Colonel Swinton believed that his battle machine would have to have tracks like a farm tractor to go across country. In October, 1914, he wrote a letter to Lord Kitchener, the head of the British Army, suggesting his idea. But neither Kitchener nor the War Department was interested.

However, the scheme reached the ears of Winston Churchill, who was then head of the British Navy and experimenting with armored cars for the Naval Brigade serving in France. Winston Churchill set up a committee of naval officers to work out a battle machine for land warfare. They tried such combinations as steam rollers, tracks, and enormous wheels, but nothing worked satisfactorily.

Finally Colonel Swinton went to France to find out what was wrong. He came back with the news that what the soldiers wanted was not a machine to carry men, but one that would destroy machine guns. By this time the army had become interested and had sent some of its officers to help on the navy's project.

One of the officers working on the project was a young lieutenant named W. G. Wilson. He was the person who suggested the first successful idea. The machine he planned was to be shaped rather like a long diamond and to have tracks that went all the way around on each side. Work was completed rapidly on this model and it was tested in February, 1915.

A hundred of the new machines had been ordered before the question of what to call them came up. The British wanted to keep them a secret in order to surprise the enemy. So they went to Colonel Swinton again because he had such a good imagination. He suggested calling the machines "tanks" so that people could be told the army was moving water tanks built for the Russians. That is how tanks got their name!

Tanks did more than anything else to win World War I. As a reward, Colonel Swinton was made a general and a knight.

8

Modern Wonders

With one exception, the most important modern inventions have been made by groups of people working in teams. Work moves rapidly because the scientists of today have learned what to look for. When there is a job to be done, they usually split the work up into parts, with different people doing the things at which they are especially good. The only inventor who has worked almost alone is Clarence Birdseye, and he did not intend to invent anything.

When Clarence Birdseye was a small boy he wanted to study animals. As a child of only five years, he gave his mother the fur of a mouse he had caught and prepared. When he went to high school in Montclair, New Jersey, he attended cooking class, partly because it would teach him more about animals and partly because he was always interested in food. After he finished high school he was able to pay his way through college for three years by selling frogs to zoos and rats to college professors. But there was not enough money to take him the rest of the way.

In 1912 Clarence Birdseye met Sir Wilfred Grenfell, the

In Labrador Clarence Birdseye found a way to freeze

famous missionary to Labrador. With the missionary's help, Birdseye went to Labrador as a fur trader, and for the next four years made trips back and forth. On one trip home he was married and his wife returned to Labrador with him.

Labrador is a very cold country, where meat is preserved by freezing it outdoors. Clarence Birdseye noticed that meat frozen on the coldest days had a better flavor than meat frozen at other times. This made him curious, so he began testing some of this meat and looking at it under the microscope.

Birdseye found that when meat was frozen slowly long thin ice needles formed in its cells and pierced the cell walls.

126

vegetables rapidly without breaking their tiny cells

When the slowly frozen meat thawed, the cells would be broken, causing a change in quality. But if the meat were frozen very fast on a very cold day, the ice crystals did not have time to build up into long needles. Then the cells were not damaged.

This gave Birdseye the idea that if he could freeze other things very rapidly, the same thing might happen. But even in Labrador there are not many days when the temperature reaches 40 or 45 degrees below zero. Some way had to be found to freeze things rapidly without waiting for the coldest days. Birdseye hit upon a plan when he remembered that salty water can get very cold without freezing. So he placed cabbages in salt water and then put them where freezing winds were blowing. The cabbages quickly froze. When Birdseye looked at them later, he found the tiny cells were not broken.

This was an important discovery because fruit and vegetable cells are usually more delicate than those in meat. But the discovery was not going to be very useful if everything had to be taken to Labrador to be frozen by the cold winds! Clarence Birdseye would have to invent a machine that would freeze foods immediately after they had been gathered. But to invent such a machine would be too costly for a man who had so little money for experiments.

At this point Birdseye was lucky. Many of the furs from Labrador come to the United States through Gloucester, Massachusetts, where he had friends. One of these men, who owned an ice plant, allowed Birdseye to use a corner of it for his experiments. Birdseye began working on a machine that used very cold salt water, with metal plates touching the food to be frozen. With borrowed money he was able to get parts made for the machine he had designed.

He was lucky to be working in the fishing community of Gloucester, for of all foods, fish is the hardest to keep fresh. So as soon as Clarence Birdseye's experiments began to succeed, he found that many Gloucester people were interested. He was able to get three men to invest money in his project as partners. They froze fish and packed it in old candy boxes.

It took some time to get stores to agree to sell the new frozen fish. But as soon as people began eating Birdseye's fish they came back for more, and it was not long before he began freezing and selling other things. Today there are stores everywhere selling frozen foods and it is possible for people to get many foods they could never get before.

After his success with his freezing machine Clarence Birdseye decided he had really wanted to be an inventor all the time. He invented heat lamps and improved electric bulbs. Then he found a new way of catching whales. Now he has more than 300 patents.

The other two inventions that are most important today sprang from the same discovery, and many people worked to perfect them. To understand this discovery, we must remember that everything is made up of chemical elements. There are a great many of these elements, but some that you will recognize are calcium, carbon, gold, iodine, sodium, and oxygen. Chemical elements, in turn, are made up of atoms. These are so tiny that they cannot be seen even with the strongest microscope.

Every atom of a chemical element behaves exactly like every other atom of that same element. That is, if you take two atoms of the element called hydrogen and one atom of the element called oxygen, the combination will be water every time.

For a long time atoms were supposed to be the smallest things there are, the building blocks out of which everything else is made up. But in 1896 a French professor named Henri Becquerel discovered something very peculiar about the element uranium, the heaviest of all elements.

Henri Becquerel himself was not a very interesting person except to other scientists. Both his grandfather and his father had been very good chemists, so when Henri Becquerel was a boy all the talk in the house was about chemistry. No one was surprised when he studied the subject and eventually became a chemistry professor. In his spare time he began experimenting with some of the chemical elements.

Becquerel found that when a piece of uranium was brought close to a photographic negative and left there for a while, even in the dark, something happened to the negative. A mark would be left on it, just as though a flash of light had struck it. Even when there was a thin sheet of metal between the uranium and the negative, the same thing happened.

Becquerel decided that the uranium must be giving off some kind of rays. After a time he was able to show that the rays were something like electricity.

Becquerel's discovery set all the chemists to working on the problem of what the rays could be. Among those who worked on it were Pierre and Marie Curie. Marie Curie was a Polish girl who had come to study in Paris, where she met and married Pierre Curie, a teacher.

While the Curies were experimenting with uranium to see what made the rays, they found that a bit of uranium ore gave off more rays than pure uranium did. The Curies decided that there must be something in the ore that gave off more rays than uranium. To find what this could be, they began to separate the ore into all the elements of which it was composed. This was a long and difficult task. In the middle of it Pierre Curie was killed by a truck but Marie Curie did not stop her work.

After years of work in which she had to handle quantities of chemicals much smaller than the point of a needle, Mme. Curie succeeded in proving that the uranium ore contained another substance. This substance proved to be a new element which Mme. Curie named radium. Later, she was able to show that radium gave off rays because it was rotting away and becoming a different element. While doing so, it was losing part of itself.

But if this were true, then atoms could not be the smallest things in existence. Atoms must be made up of other parts still smaller! It was not long before several scientists were able to prove that this was so.

In the center of every atom there is a kind of heart called the nucleus. Spinning round and round it like planets around the sun are very much tinier particles called electrons. The odd part of it is that some of these electrons can be drawn away from the atom for a time by strong electrical charges.

This last fact led to another great invention. It was made by Lee DeForest, who grew up in Alabama, where his father was president of a college. Near DeForest's boyhood home there was a big furnace which interested him so much that he spent hours watching it. Finally he built a model of it. When he was ten or eleven, his father took him to a factory where locomotives were repaired. Lee DeForest went home and built a large model locomotive in his backyard. When he was 13 he decided he was going to be an inventor, and after he got out of college he began inventing at once. His first invention was a new kind of bicycle, but this was not a success.

In order to earn a living while he was beginning to invent things, Lee DeForest went to work for an electrical company. What he learned on his new job gave him the idea that there was more room for inventions in electricity than in any other field. Some of his first work was in improving the wireless telegraph, which Marconi had only just invented.

In 1900 Lee DeForest began experimenting to determine if there were wireless signals in the air. The device he used had an electric spark which jumped across a gap. As he worked, DeForest noticed that every time the spark jumped, the gaslight overhead became dim and then brightened again. It was not hard to figure out that this was caused by sound waves from the spark. But it made DeForest ask himself: "What if you could make an electric light dim and brighten by jumping a spark at it?"

This started him on a long series of experiments which are much too complicated to tell about here. It took him years of experimentation to discover that when there are two filaments instead of one inside the bulb and the current flows from one to the other, some of the electrons jump across.

This was what he needed to know. Then he thought of putting between the two filaments something called a grid. A strong current flows through the tube. But if there is a very weak current on the grid it will behave like a stop sign and not let the electrons or the current pass. So the tube will really make a very weak difference in current into a strong one by making the weak current control the strong one.

DeForest called the tube in which he did this the Audion. It was patented in 1907 and it was one of the most useful patents ever given. All sorts of uses were found for DeForest's Audion tube. They are employed in radar, which enables us to see through smoke or thick fog by means of tiny electrical waves that bounce off anything solid. Audion tubes are also used in wireless telephones, in television, and in talking movies. Lee DeForest had a great deal to do with inventing all these things.

The other great invention that came out of Mme. Curie's discovery is atomic energy. After she found out about radium, several other elements were discovered that came apart by themselves, including one of the two kinds of uranium. When an atom of an element does this, it not only turns into something else, but it gives off a great deal of energy. It is a little like the burning of a lump of coal, in which is stored some of the energy that came from the sun thousands of years ago.

But one atom of an element is so very small that the energy given off as it decays does not amount to much. Then, too, a lump of such a substance takes a long time to wear away. If you had a pound of radium it would be 1590 years before even half of it had changed into something else!

When it was discovered that atoms decay, many people thought that if a method could be found to make a large number of atoms decay at the same time, the energy could be used. The amount of energy released would be far beyond that released by burning coal or oil, or even the most powerful explosives. Scientists in many countries worked on the problem and wrote back and forth to each other as their work progressed. It would not be fair to say that any one of them solved it alone. But the most important work was done by Enrico Fermi.

Like many inventors, Fermi became interested in his future career while he was still a small boy. Born in Rome, Italy, he was studying physics and mathematics at an age when most boys are just beginning to read. When he was thirteen an engineer who was a friend of his father's taught him mathematics in the evening. During his eighteenth year, Enrico Fermi won a scholarship at the University of Pisa. Later he received scholarships to other European colleges, and before long he was giving lectures himself. Not long afterward, he came to America, for he did not like the government that had started to rule Italy.

In the United States Enrico Fermi was quickly made Professor of Physics at Columbia University, where he began to experiment with atoms. He learned a great deal about what held them together and what breaks them up. When the second World War started, Fermi was considered one of the best atomic scientists in the country. For this reason he was chosen as a leading member of what was called Manhattan Project.

By this time scientists had learned that some atoms could be broken up if they were bombarded with tiny fragments of other atoms. Now, if an atom of some element could be made to split into the right kind of fragments, and these fragments started other atoms breaking up and these, in turn, set off still others, soon all the atoms in this piece of the element would be breaking up. This is known as a "chain reaction." The explosion that would result would be many times greater than any that had ever been seen on earth.

Now this was still theory. Nobody knew quite what element to use or how to get enough of them together. Nobody knew how to start the explosion off without blowing up everything else around.

Then things began to happen quickly after the Japanese attack on Pearl Harbor. We were in the war, and had to do everything possible to defend ourselves. We knew we were in real danger when it became known that our enemies were also working on the problem of an atomic explosion. We were determined that they should not get it first and use it on us.

So the government set up Manhattan Project to look into the whole question of atomic explosions. Directing the project was a scientist named J. Robert Oppenheimer who was born in New York City and whose life was strangely like that of Enrico Fermi. Oppenheimer began as a student who never seemed to be able to get enough of mathematics and physics. After he went to college he began to win scholarships, some of them to the very colleges in Europe that Enrico Fermi had attended.

When Oppenheimer returned to this country he became a professor at California Institute of Technology and an atomic scientist. He was chosen to be the head of Manhattan Project partly because of his scientific knowledge, and partly because he got along so well with people that other scientists liked to work with him.

He set up Manhattan Project in a room beneath a football stadium in Chicago. It was there that scientists began to look for something they might never find.

Of course, Oppenheimer and Fermi were not the only members of the project. All over the country dozens of scientists were working on details of splitting the atom. No great invention ever took so many people or had so many difficulties to overcome. Just how they found the answer to the problem is still a secret, but Enrico Fermi and the others finally succeeded in making an atomic bomb. The first one was exploded at White Sands, New Mexico, on July 16, 1945.

After it had gone off the scientists began to discover that they had invented a lot more than a tremendous explosion. They found other atoms that would break up, and some of these proved to be useful to doctors and other scientists. It was also discovered that some atoms could be made to break up fast enough to give a great deal of heat but not fast enough for an explosion. This means that atomic furnaces can be used to drive engines and make electricity. Some day, perhaps, atomic energy will make it possible for us to get along without burning coal or oil.

In fact, we do not yet know all the things that atomic power and broken atoms can do for us. Probably the use of these atoms will be the richest source of new inventions for many years to come. Besides furnishing power it has already been discovered that many of them are useful in curing diseases. There are possibilities that others will make plants grow better and richer.

But this is not the only type of invention we may expect to see. Engineers in Italy and Iceland have succeeded in putting the hot springs of those countries to work to make electricity. In Boston, a house has been built which stores up the heat it gets from the sun in summer and gives it out again in winter without needing any furnace. A North African has invented a stove that runs on the heat of the sun and may be used to run an engine. Botanists are inventing new kinds of plants that will grow better and produce more food. New kinds of cloth are being made from plastics, lasting longer than those of cotton or wool.

Most of these do not yet count as real inventions because they need to be perfected before everyone can use them. But they give an idea of a few of the things we can still expect from inventors.

Index